D1084992

MOSCOW DIARY

Published in the United States
by DUFOUR EDITIONS, INC.
Chester Springs. Pa. 19425

© *Ampersand Ltd.*

Printed in Great Britain for Ampersand, Ltd., 199, Piccadilly, London,
W.1., by Williams, Lea and Company Limited, Clifton House,
Worship Street, London, E.C.2.

First Published 1961

MOSCOW DIARY

Francis Sejersted

CONTENTS

FOREWORD

The train gathered speed out of Oslo and the winter barrenness of our Norwegian countryside spread out on either side in bleak panorama. We realised suddenly it would be some months before we saw the familiar contours of our homeland again, and nostalgia travelled with us. We tried to relax, but we were too excited.

And then—as though for the first time—we became conscious of the weight of our responsibility. If we hadn't felt it before it came to us very forcibly at that moment. My friend Ingjald, a fellow student from Oslo University, and I looked at each other— saying nothing but both of us wondering what we had let ourselves in for.

There was good reason to feel excited. We were the first Norwegian students to be setting out for Moscow University in nearly four years. We were to pioneer a new era in Norwegian-Soviet student relationships—that was the responsibility we felt then.

The last students from Norway who travelled this route, feeling maybe as tense and excited as we were, had preceded the Hungarian uprising in 1956, when the world was horrified by the news of Soviet tanks crushing the people of Budapest.

Norwegian reactions had been the same as everyone else's in the West; the same horror and anger that a powerful nation which boasted of its anti-colonialist feeling should stifle an ambition for independence in such a ruthless way as it did in Hungary. We remembered that Hungarian students were among those who demanded freedom, and were answered with Russian bullets.

Our Student Council promptly suspended the student exchange programme in protest. And it had taken nearly four years to pick up the threads of our relationships. Ingjald and I had been selected to represent the Norwegian student body in bridging these years of silence.

The date was January 31, 1960.

We were heading for Stockholm, thence across the Baltic to Helsinki. Soon we would cross the Finnish-Soviet frontier and step down at Viborg for the first time on Soviet soil. From there by rail to Leningrad, where the fabulous winter palace of the Tsars is a permanent reminder of old Russia, and finally to Moscow—to the huge white stone colossus of the University which towers above Lenin Hills.

Beyond Kalinin and the silver thread of the Volga our train would wander through a flat, grey country —endless vistas dotted with humble cottages that seemed to illustrate Chuchev's expression "the homeland of long-suffering".

I also thought of Dostoievsky's *The House of the Dead:* "Here there is a world apart, unlike everything else . . . life as nowhere else and a people apart".

It is this corner apart that I am going to describe.

I started a diary a few days after I arrived in Moscow. I wanted to remember all the people I met, what they said, all the things Ingjald and I did together and the places we visited. I had no thought in mind that it might eventually interest a publisher. It was a purely personal record.

I wanted to preserve those experiences in Moscow —especially the nights we spent in our rooms talking politics with Russian friends, trying to get under their guard to find out what the Russian student is really like, what his problems and his ambitions are.

We know little about Russian young people except the picture we get from the propaganda handouts—the inevitable collective picture of bright-eyed young Communists full of social consciousness working on the Socialist transformation. I was meeting individuals, and for all their Communist veneer they had the minds of individualists.

They were hospitable, generous, and intelligent. Often they were eager for news of life outside their own environment, and they wanted it at first hand rather than through the tedious Russian newspapers.

But the standards they had, and the bases on which they argued with us, had obviously been deeply ingrained. They had no method of judging their standards against those of other people. Something was missing . . . and I suspect it was reliable information about how the other half lives.

Politically, most of the young people seemed passive. They had given up trying to resist the pressures of the society in which they lived and had become submissive to any new edicts. They questioned whether one had the *right* to choose one's ideology.

In many ways the Russians with whom we had those nightly discussions were at an advantage. They were talking in their native language. But it was useful for us, too. It meant we heard things spontaneously; a direct communion of minds unhampered by the serious obstacles of language. Probably if we had not spoken Russian we would have come away with far less appreciation of the Russian temperament. We might have found them shy and awkward, which would have given us a completely wrong impression.

For us it was good practice. Yet the main

problem was trying to arrive at some common definition of the lingual and political terms we used to each other. After a time we found out in what way we could evoke responses. For example, we would hold up a discussion while we asked for definitions of certain words they used so frequently —words like "peace" and "freedom". Then we found they would sometimes quote familiar propaganda lines, as though from a book of poetry.

Despite the difficulties, we came to grips with problems that occupy the minds of young people all over the world, even if our concepts were poles apart.

The thing that seemed to give our Russian friends the most amusement was the fact that I was a Conservative—a party card holder and ex-chairman of the Conservative Students' Association in Oslo. I made no attempt to disguise the fact. Indeed, this was one of the first things the Soviet authorities wanted to know. It seemed that Russian students had never met anyone with such strange ideas before! But it didn't stop any of them seeking me out to discuss their problems and to ask about young people in Norway.

Ingjald, a Socialist, fared little better than I in the political esteem of Russian students. Social Democracy seems to be a naughty word to Communists . . . at least, so my Russian friends would say.

It is hard to generalise about such a big country, for there are always contradictions. But the students I met—and I'm sure they were representative— were as inquisitive and idealistic as students in any other part of the world, and as for their political background, I couldn't escape the thought that if I lived under those conditions, and faced the same pressures every day, I would act in a similar way and hold similar opinions. One's attitude must be relative to the society in which one lives.

I did not meet one Russian student who was prepared to be a martyr to causes of which he had little understanding anyway.

Like students everywhere, the Russians soon tire of having politics thrust at them. They would show their feelings in no uncertain terms towards lectures or propaganda demonstrations that bored them. They played truant from lectures, and once I saw students slow-handclap a party of tiresome propagandists off a platform. I didn't blame them in the least, for it was one of those interminable "Let Us Be Good Socialist Workers" performances. As far as I know there were no reprisals against the students.

It seemed inevitable that we would go to Russia full of suspicions. So many stories have filtered back home over the years of Russian methods of keeping tabs on people. I could prove nothing, but the suspicions remained with me during the whole of my stay; uneasy feelings that I could not explain or substantiate that we were being watched or overheard.

Ingjald and I felt so uneasy about the prospect of outsiders listening in to our private conversations that sometimes our voices would drop, quite involuntarily, to a conspiratorial whisper; or again we would make some derogatory remark in a loud voice and shout at the walls: "Did you hear that?" This became a kind of joke with us.

One day we even went round the room tapping on the walls to see if we could trace those hidden microphones! We found nothing; we could prove nothing. In most cases I suppose our suspicions were groundless. But all the time we had the feeling that this was a police State, and we were foreigners in it.

I have often heard criticism from foreign students who have been to Moscow, and from Press reports, that attempts are made to indoctrinate them.

We found no special efforts were made to indoctrinate *us*. Yet indoctrination was all round, and it was relentless. As foreigners we were merely observing something that is part and parcel of the Soviet educational system. Indoctrination cannot be divorced from that system, and it certainly could not be expected that Soviet educationists would depart from their Marxist beliefs in the case of foreigners.

Certainly there is indoctrination, and foreign students Moscow-bound should realise that it goes with the system. We sat with Russian students at lectures containing definite Marxist-Leninist slants. I cannot believe this was specially laid on to indoctrinate us, but was the routine treatment of subjects in order to give a constant political guidance to students, irrespective of what nationalities happened to be in the class.

Our meetings with the head of the Foreign Bureau at the University illustrated the intransigence of Russian official thinking. He gave us fatherly talks about the shortcomings of the capitalist system and the peaceful policies of the Soviet Union.

While we were in Moscow the Russians shot down the American U2 aircraft, and we became directly involved in an international incident since it seemed the plane might be heading for Norway. The Foreign Bureau official became very awkward about some travel arrangements we were making and reminded us that this incident showed the aggressiveness of the West. I am at a loss to know why our personal travel arrangements should have been linked with the shooting down of an American plane, but to the official Russian mind it seemed we were personally responsible for the attitude of the Norwegian Government towards this incident, and the political repercussions were being scaled down to our level in upsetting our travel plans.

Despite some unpleasantness with Soviet official-dom, which we sometimes found would react to our advantage if we made an unholy row, and in spite of constant astonishment at the way the Russians put up with shoddy service in their shops, we spent some happy times in Moscow.

For five months it was our home. They were months packed with excitement and interest—and not a little work. We came away with a new appre-ciation of our fellow students in Russia, many of whom we regard as permanent friends.

Certainly it is important that we should continue to engage in student exchange programmes with the Communist countries. They are eager to get to know us, and I believe that through exchanging ideas and discussing our mutual problems we might yet arrive at some common definition of that much-used term—"peaceful co-existence".

But these are reflections. On the train from Oslo that morning of January 31 we were travelling into a largely unknown and infinitely mysterious world which for years had sealed itself off from contact with us.

So let's go back and turn the pages of my Moscow diary, to peer behind the curtain at student life on the Lenin Hills.

F.S.

Oslo, 1961

THE MOSCOW SCENE

Thursday, February 4, 1960

At last I can settle down to write some notes after a few hectic days of travelling, seeing people, filling forms and making arrangements. We are here in Moscow, at any rate. After arriving in Leningrad we took a taxi to the Embassy and from there went straight to the Student Council of the Youth Committee in central Moscow, as instructed. This was the Committee which had invited us through the student exchange programme with Oslo. Most things about the atmosphere and set-up reminded us of home—pleasant and informal. We had the feeling that we were a little unexpected and regrets were expressed that they hadn't met us at the station. We said it was not their fault—how could they have known when we were going to arrive, especially after we had changed our plan to travel by rail instead of by plane from Leningrad?

With a plump Russian student named Alexei, who had been instructed by the Student Council to look after us, we went to the Foreign Bureau. This was done with some difficulty—Alexei had obviously never been there before.

At the bureau we met three Russians, Alexeev, who didn't open his mouth once, Mozolin, a lively character who did most of the talking and was evidently head of the office, and Tokmakov, who backed up Mozolin. Tokmakov was apparently Secretary of the Faculty of Philology at Moscow University.

The conversation was not particularly pleasant. The Russians obviously wanted to know what we intended to do in the Soviet Union. We stated firmly that first of all we wanted to study the language and at the same time get to know local conditions. I added that I also wanted to attend certain lectures on literary subjects if there was time, and that I would like to know what lectures were being given. The Russians were unable to give me this information, but they continued to probe into our plans. Finally, as far as I was concerned, it was agreed that I should concentrate on the classical period. I was to ring Tokmakov the next day to make arrangements to meet the Dean.

Before leaving, incidentally, we had to fill in a form asking, among other things, the social status of our parents, what our fathers did, and to what political party we belonged. After a little hesitation we answered. To the political question I wrote boldly: "Conservative", and waited for some reaction. There was none.

We went by Metro to the University on the Lenin Hills, still accompanied by Alexei, who appeared to be even less at home there than he did in the previous building. The Metro looked like a throw-back to Victoriana, with very ornate stations.

After a lot of wandering around the University we found our way to the office we were looking for —in the cellar. There we were issued with the necessary documents and had to register at the University. Once again we had to fill in a detailed form, but the question about political affiliations was crossed out. We handed over five passport photographs (yes, five!), and were given in return a provisional pass. We are to collect the proper pass, together with our residence permit, in two weeks' time. I can't imagine why they want five passport photographs. It will be interesting to see if I get any of them back. Finally, we were given a room in the

Sejersted stands on a ledge overlooking a grey Caucasian valley. Below: General view of Tiflis, crowned by an ancient fortress.

16

guest wing of the University, which Ingjald and I are to share for three or four days, it seems quite good, apart from being awfully cold and draughty.

We were half-dead with hunger from going around all day without a bite, and no one had thought to mention food. Anyway we finally staggered down to the students' restaurant in the cellar, where we had some kind of meat pie with rice—very good. The restaurant was large and cold, but otherwise not bad at all. Afterwards we collected our baggage from the Embassy.

Friday, February 5

I telephoned Tokmakov, as agreed, but apparently the Dean is unable to receive me until after the weekend. Tokmakov promised to ring me. Mean-

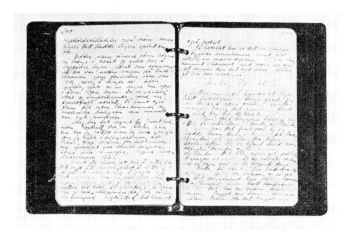

Photograph of the original diary

while, however, we had called on Nikoforov, head of the Foreign Bureau in the Lenin Hills, who had asked for us. He occupies a very nice office on the ninth floor of the main section of the building. On first acquaintance he seemed to be pleasant and straight-forward, though perhaps a little too smooth. After our rather unpleasant discussion of the previous day with Mozolin, it was a nice surprise to find Nikoforov fully understanding what we wanted to do.

He said he thought that one of the most important tasks was for us to become accustomed to local conditions and get to know Soviet students. We asked about travel possibilities. He said he would do his utmost for us.

Then he spoke of peace and friendship, and said we would have many subjects for discussion with Soviet students—even though we might not see eye to eye over certain matters. He mentioned the North Atlantic Treaty Organisation as an example.

Saturday, February 6

I am writing this in the guest house lounge—having been driven out of my room by the cold, even though it is not more than 15°C outside. We have enough blankets, but I suppose I am feeling the cold more because I have been used to better built houses in Norway. We have been promised single rooms, so I am hoping things will improve.

When we got back from a visit to the city around 9.30 last night we tried to get some food. But the restaurant was having a so-called "hygiene day", which meant it was closed for cleaning. It seems that on hygiene days the students are expected to find a cheap restaurant somewhere in the district, but we don't know where these are yet. We managed to find a little cafeteria type of place elsewhere in the cellar, but had difficulty in ordering as we did not understand the terms on the menu. It turned out to be some kind of special food.

This morning I went off to greet some Western student colleagues, and met a Danish civil engineer who had already arrived for the autumn term to study electronic computers. He had run into trouble as soon as he arrived. First, nobody seemed to know he was coming and least of all what to do with him. He was put into an old students' home in the middle of Moscow, where he shared a room with three others. Then he was told that foreigners were not permitted to study electronic computers. He was later transferred to a single room in the Faculty of Philology on the Lenin Hills.

In the meantime he had been improving his Russian but had had little to do with electronic computers. In fact he had not seen a single machine, though he'd read a little theory. He told me he had a Russian friend who wanted to learn Danish. The Russian had been able to get hold of an electronic computer for translating purposes. In the opinion of my Danish friend the Russians are well ahead of everybody else in the sphere of translating by electronic means. Unfortunately he had no further information.

We had lunch today in the so-called "professors' restaurant". This was much nicer than the students' restaurant—and about twice as expensive. We talked trivialities at our table with a student of geography.

Monday, February 8

My birthday! Ingjald congratulated me, but otherwise I let it pass. On Saturday evening (February 6) we went to a kind of social evening in the "Cultural Wing". First there was a dance in a large, marble decorated and pillared hall. The orchestra, which sat at one end around a statue of Gorki, consisted of a saxophone, a drum and an accordion. It played rather antiquated dance music— a mixture of waltzes and old fashioned jazz.

The whole set-up was fairly mixed. All kinds of dress was on show and many different nationalities were represented. A few of the girls would not have looked out of place in Norway, but generally the standard of the women was low, though quite a number of them were made up in the Western style.

After a good half-hour's dancing we went into a very beautiful theatre which quickly filled up almost to bursting point. We sat there waiting endlessly, while the students showed their impatience by slow handclapping. Finally seven men and women workers trooped onto the stage and sat at a round table. They were introduced in turn, and then it was announced that they were members of labour brigades which had won the title "Brigade of Communist Labour".

One of the women began to talk. She spoke clearly and I could follow what she was saying. But how tedious she became! She produced masses of statistics and explained laboriously how her brigade had determined to achieve the title "Brigade of Communist Labour". Then when she sat down one of the male workers promptly got up and lectured with equal tedium and length. It was obvious that the audience was bored to tears. The students became increasingly noisy and finally the worker's speech was drowned by slow handclapping. It was quite impossible for him to be heard above the racket, so the whole troupe had to leave the stage. It looked like a propaganda demonstration put on primarily for the benefit of the Russian students.

Things were better once the labour brigade had gone. There was a variety show by amateurs from the Likhachev factory—of varied quality but some of the performers were really first-class.

Tuesday, February 9

On Saturday we went with a group of students, including Russians, to the Technical Museum. Our Danish friend came along, too, and I had a chat with a little Mongolian who was studying Caucasian languages. At the museum the main emphasis was on sputniks of all kinds and a vast horde of people listened intently to the guide. We also saw lots of radios, TV sets, tape recorders and so on. I was prevailed upon to record a few words in Norwegian.

During the afternoon I met a Danish girl student, Anne-Marie, who was rather sweet and charming. Her main interest was Slavonic history. She had studied Russian for only three months before coming to Moscow, but had a good knowledge of Czech and Polish. She told me she had been given a teacher to herself at the Institute of Languages.

It seemed she had not been interrogated to the same extent as we had when she arrived in Moscow, and she spoke very nicely about Messrs Tokmakov and Mozolin of the Foreign Bureau. She, Ingjald and I went out to dinner together. In the restaurant she introduced us to a friendly student from West Germany, and we ended up the day by going to his place with a bottle of cognac. He talked of a very interesting trip he had made to Jaroslav, Vladimir and Ivanovo. It had required a good deal of trouble and effort to get this trip organised, he said, but finally it had come off.

He told us of the unbelievably low standard of living in these towns. Even among the so-called intelligentsia there was widespread dirtiness and frightful overcrowding. He said that in one town of about 200,000 inhabitants there was only one water main on the main street. It had been a depressing but illuminating tour. It had taught him that Moscow was one thing—and Russia quite another.

He also told us that he had had two rolls of film confiscated and destroyed by the police—having been caught photographing slums. When he protested that he only wanted to get an objective picture of the Soviet Union, the police retorted that in that case he ought to have been photographing the fine new houses of culture. etc.

On Monday morning we took the initiative ourselves to get something done about our rooms and studies. First I went into town to see Tokmakov. He was most accommodating and promptly arranged for me to meet Samarin, the Dean, a charming chap. After a short talk, he and Tokmakov agreed that I should have a tutor (rukovoditch), who would help me at the University. Tokmakov also arranged for Ingjald and myself next day to visit the Language Institute for Foreigners—housed on the fourth floor of the Zoological Museum.

Wednesday, February 10

Today we went to the Foreign Bureau to organise our student grant. There we talked with Alexeev, who was quite charming this time and straight away arranged our first month's money—900 roubles. He also presented us with complimentary tickets to some kind of performance at the "House of Friendship" in the city. Unfortunately we had no time to use them.

Back in the Lenin Hills, we sought out Nikoforov to find out when we could move into rooms of our own. At the same time we stressed that to improve our Russian and to get to know some of the local people we would each like to share a room with a Russian student. Nikoforov said he would do his best and asked us to call back later and have a word with his secretary, Igor Mikhailovich.

When we returned we met a tall, dark and very young lad who announced himself as Igor Mikhailovich. He had never heard of us and advised us to call back between 3 and 4 p.m. Once again we explained that we would like to share rooms with some Russians, and Igor promised to do his best. When we called on him again everything had been fully organised. Just a couple of snags. We had asked to live with Russians. We were being put in the same block. We had asked to be put among lawyers and language students. We were being sent to the physics wing.

Naturally I asked why we had been put together, and whether it would be possible to change the arrangement to enable us to get better acquainted with fellow Russian students. Quite impossible, said Igor Mikhailovich. Unfortunately there was no other accommodation available at present, and no changes could be made in the middle of a semester.

When we moved in we talked with students in the same corridor. They laughed when we told them no other rooms were free. They promptly showed us three empty rooms on the floor below and said that a Russian and a Chinese student who were then on vacation would shortly be moving back into the room alloted to us!

Once we had been issued with a room there began an endless series of visits to various offices. First to the Passport Bureau, which was responsible for registering our new address; then to the Accounts Department to pay for the room; then to the Permit Bureau to collect our permits. This office was closed when we succeeded in tracking it down. Next we had to return to the Passport Bureau to collect the necessary authority to occupy our new quarters. According to the rules we had to have a permit before the moving in authority could be given. We were lucky. The Bureau actually issued the authority without the permit!

With everything settled we began to move, only to find that the officer in charge of our floor had left his post. We were in no mood to trifle by this time. After creating a tremendous scene we managed to get hold of the night watchman for the whole sector, who undertook to let us into the rooms and issue us with sheets and a single blanket. The remaining furnishings, including such items as a lamp, blanket, etc., we were to receive the next day.

In spite of all the formalities, we were greatly cheered by the atmosphere among the students in the Common Room on our floor. They were as helpful as they could be. One asked Ingjald where we came from. On being told Norway he brightened up at once and in a rather relieved voice declared:

"And we thought you were Czechs or Poles!" It seemed that the Russian students weren't especially keen on the East Europeans. They regarded them as being too proud; too retiring. They were more enthusiastic at being able to meet some Western students.

Yesterday morning we visited the Institute for Foreign Students—the Language Institute—and received a most friendly reception from a lady named Roshkova, who gave us the task of writing in Russian an account of our own country. It was to be completed in 40 minutes. While Madame Roshkova corrected my essay, I dropped in on Tokmakov again and was told to call next day to be introduced to my Cicerone—the lecturer Pustavoyt. Then I went back to Madame Roshkova, who had finished correcting the work. Phew! The result left a lot to be desired. It was decided that Ingjald and I would be in the same group and have at least four two-hour Russian language lessons a week. We were asked to return the following day to meet our teacher, Olga Rassodova, and to make arrangements with her about times and dates.

Last night we were invited by our Danish girl friend, Anne Marie, to call on some medical students from Ghana. They served us Russian slivovits and we had a jolly evening. Politics were hardly mentioned, though it wasn't hard to see the Ghanaians were certainly not Communists.

This morning we went back to the Language Institute and made the necessary arrangements with Madame Rassodova, who seemed a nice person. Then I registered at the library (more forms). Later in the day we called in to see Tokmakov, but unfortunately my director of studies had not arrived. We waited for three quarters of an hour in vain.

*In the poorer districts a newspaper posted in a glass
case (above) keeps the people abreast of the party's
latest achievements. (Taken in Tiflis)*

In the meantime, however, Tokmakov and I chatted. He asked about Norway—first about its nature and then about its standard of living, with particular emphasis on housing. Nothing appeared to surprise him particularly (naturally I don't know if he believed what I told him). We went on to talk of Sweden and its unusually high standard of living.

Then Tokmakov made a curious observation. He said he had read somewhere that Sweden had the highest suicide rate in the world, and asked me whether in my opinion this had something to do with the "idleness" of youth there. We finally agreed that material wealth is not the only goal in life, but that one must also strive for higher things.

Rather abstract, but this was the first time I had discussed anything with Tokmakov and was a little unsure of my ground.

Before leaving it was agreed I should meet Pustavoyt, on Friday after my language lesson.

Friday, February 12

Yesterday we got into conversation with one of the American students in the restaurant. He introduced us to a Russian student of architecture who had very strong views about Ibsen, the Norwegian dramatist. It was Ibsen's early realistic drama that interested him in particular, and not so much his more famous symbolistic dramas.

In the evening we tried to get in to see a West German film running at the University cinema. It was called something like: "I Seek You". We sought in vain, because all the seats were sold. It was sold out again to more successful seekers than we.

Today we had our first Russian lesson. Our

teacher, Rassodova, seemed agreeable and efficient. Then we went once again to see Tokmakov, but there was still no sign of Pustavoyt. We waited another three-quarters of an hour, and finally he showed up. Pustavoyt turned out to be very affable. He advised me to attend his lectures, and in addition we agreed to meet for an hour once a fortnight to discuss certain books which I would study in advance.

When I got back to my room the corridor watchman had fixed gummed paper strips around the cracks in the windows. The draught has been pretty fearsome, but I am hoping for better things now!

Saturday, February 13

This morning there was a long queue in front of the newspaper kiosk on the first floor. I can't understand why anyone should want to stand in a queue just to get hold of those tedious Russian newspapers.

Afterwards I went to my first lecture in Auditorium 66. Pustavoyt was talking about Hertzen, the writer. He turned out to be quite an orator and consequently Hertzen was praised to the skies. The lecture, however, was based on an article on Hertzen by Lenin, and Hertzen's work was carefully interpreted to follow the doctrinaire line. For instance, when Hertzen had used the word "realism" he had naturally meant "materialism". We also heard that Hertzen's democratic ideas were not mere "bourgeois democratic ideas but *real* democratic, that is, revolutionary, ideas". Pustavoyt "proved" this by quoting extensively how Hertzen had loved the people.

I suppose this was a sample of the indoctrination one can expect in Soviet teaching. But merely by *being* in the Soviet Union one is inevitably exposed to it. The system operates on this basis.

After the lecture I started talking to one of the students, Peter. He was enamoured neither of Hertzen nor Pustavoyt. The really great Russian critic, he declared, was Belinski. Hertzen wasn't fit to lick his boots. Then the conversation got on to Dostoievsky, whose works Peter obviously knew well.

I sounded him out as discreetly as I could about student grants, remembering that our allowance had amounted to 900 roubles for the month. If I understood him correctly, he enjoyed a basic grant of 320 roubles a month. This sum could be augmented if he did well at examinations. But some students received no financial support whatever—for example those whose family income averaged 600 roubles per member a month.

It seemed by comparison that we were receiving a very fair allowance. It enabled us to buy things that Russian students would find difficult, though many of them were getting a little money from home to help out. I imagine they could manage fairly well with a little support from home. But with just a basic allowance they must have a rather lean time. I have come across no resentment among Russian students that foreigners seem to be getting allowances so much higher.

According to Peter, most students in their third year are allowed to move into the new students' house in the Lenin Hills. Peter himself was in the second year at the Faculty of Philology and lived in a six-man students' room at Sokolniki on the other side of Moscow. He also spent some time with his mother, who had a little house outside the city.

Before coming to Moscow Peter had lived with his family in Perm, where he had attended the University. He said that the atmosphere at Moscow University was entirely different from that of Perm. Moscow University had certain liberal traditions—a lasting breath of the liberal intelligentsia of the last century.

We also talked a little about Norway and Scandinavia. Peter said that a Russian had written recently that immorality was rife in Sweden. He was fully conscious of the fact that Sweden had a very high standard of living, and wondered if there was a connection. I cannot imagine why Peter should link immorality with a high standard of living, for he evidently believed that no matter how high a standard of living was achieved in Russia, immorality would not be a feature of it. I would like to have discussed this further, but at this point he had to go to a group meeting so we couldn't finish the conversation.

Tuesday, February 16

At lunch on Sunday (February 14) we sat down alongside two Russian students. Each of them had five empty beer bottles on the table. When we got talking they appeared very interested when they learned that we were Norwegians, and gave us three bottles of beer each. Then they became very talkative—especially one who was a geographer specialising in the northern area. The other student made obvious efforts to restrain him, but he told us quite frankly he was no Communist. On the other hand he believed in the Russian people and in the need for them to make a tremendous effort to speed up their development. Three hundred years of Tartar rule, he declared, had set back Russia's development 300 years.

I asked him whether Communism was to his mind the best system to achieve this aim. He didn't answer directly, but said the Russian people needed a religion. And Communism, like Christianity or Islam, was a religion.

He was well informed about Norway and Norwegian Arctic exploration, and we suggested he should pay a visit to Norway himself some day. To this he replied that it was completely out of the question—he belonged to the common people. When we asked if he thought even "common people" would one day be able to travel abroad he replied: "Yes".

Yesterday we paid a call on the Norwegian Ambassador, Gundersen, who gave us much helpful advice. In the afternoon we met Mr. and Mrs. Karl Kramer, an American student couple. He was on an exchange scholarship, studying Russian literature, and was a little more *au fait* than I with the set-up, so could give me a number of tips.

The daily routine—at least for five days a week—appears to be homework in the morning, probably followed by a lecture and a language lesson at 3 p.m. This is what happened today—Tuesday. During a pause in Pustavoyt's lecture I talked to Peter again. I also noticed that there was a large majority of girls at the lecture—typical of the Faculty of Philology, according to Peter. In fact, he told me, for some courses only 20 per cent of the students were boys. The reason was that a scientific education offered bigger and better possibilities afterwards; and since the girls were usually less up to the mark, most of them read philology. It was difficult to get regular jobs after studying this subject, he said—one could of course become a teacher, but the majority wanted something different. Peter said there were about 1,000 students in the Faculty, not counting those who studied history, or the evening students who, I gathered, numbered as many as the regular ones.

Peter asked a few questions about conditions in Oslo, and seemed to find it odd that there was a Theological Faculty at our University. He mentioned that the lecture hall next door had formerly belonged to the Theological Faculty, and had not been changed since. When we parted after the lecture, Peter had to go on to compulsory gymnastic lessons.

In the evening we had a visit from Sasha Sorokin, a representative of the Youth Committee. He was particularly responsible for the Scandinavian Sector and it was in this capacity that he had called to see how we were getting along and whether we had been properly welcomed. [The Youth Committee is responsible for the student exchange scheme with Norway].

Sorokin referred to the difficulties about student exchanges as a result of the Hungarian uprising. He was a fervent Communist, solid as they come. He reiterated all the propaganda lines on Hungary. He knew a great deal about the internal affairs of the Norwegian student world, too. He told us he received copies of Norwegian student publications (we couldn't find out whether these were in Russian or Norwegian, but Sorokin spoke some Norwegian). When we asked about Soviet students going to Norway he replied that it was handled by the Ministry.

Thursday, February 18

Yesterday we went to a meeting given by the Norwegian-Russian Society to commemorate the 50th anniversary of the death of Ole Bull, a famous Norwegian violinist and composer. There we met two students from the Institute of Foreign Languages —Volodya and Sasha (who spoke good Norwegian).

The meeting took place in the handsome "Friendship House" in the centre of town, with about 60 people present. We were warmly greeted by the Institute's Secretary General. Someone also came from the Norwegian Embassy, and the three of us were called on by name and applauded at the beginning of the meeting. A short talk on Ole Bull was followed by a concert of Norwegian music.

During the meeting an elderly woman spoke to us in very broken Norwegian. She said she was from the Norwegian Department of Moscow Radio and would like to see us again for an interview. I replied —in the nicest possible way—that we were not too interested since we regarded these Norwegian broadcasts as one-sided and of a propaganda nature. She was in no way put out, and readily continued to talk Norwegian to us.

Saturday, February 20

Today I'm gasping—having climbed the whole

14 floors to our rooms! Despite the fact that there are three lifts going flat out in this block, you have to wait some time to get into one, and literally have to fight your way in every time. Each lift has a capacity of 18 persons, which means there are seldom fewer than 25 students at a time.

Yesterday I went on a shopping spree to get in a supply of food, having discovered that one meal a day should be eaten in one's room for two very good reasons—to avoid queuing everywhere and to save money. It's a depressing experience shopping in Moscow. Hordes of people everywhere, long queues, and bad-tempered shop assistants. Furthermore, Russians dislike giving change. Either they round off the sum to the nearest rouble, or give change in kind. Today, for example, I wanted to buy a loaf costing 1.35 roubles. Just one loaf. I handed over two rouble notes and received not only the loaf I had requested, but a smaller one as well which cost 65 kopecks.

There was an interesting little incident during the interval of Pustavoyt's lecture in the afternoon. A tough looking old hag got onto the dais and announced herself as the inspector of second year students. She said she wanted to tell those present a few home truths, and went on to complain that practically everyone had skipped the first compulsory lecture that day—a session on modern Russian. Only 15 out of the whole course had attended and it wasn't good enough, she said. This caused more merriment than soul-searching among the students, and there was even greater mirth when a roll-call showed that a good number of students were also missing from this lecture, too. Someone shouted that they were probably all sick!

I asked Peter what would happen to the absentees.

He said nothing would happen—things were pretty happy-go-lucky at Moscow University. On the other hand most other universities were a great deal tougher and would not allow this sort of thing to go on unpunished. At Moscow University, however, the offence had to be pretty serious before it met with reprisals. In general punishment would take the form of a fine of half a month's pay. I thought that in view of the smallness of the student's pay this must be quite heavy punishment.

When I asked Peter why so many students stayed away from the lectures on modern Russian he replied that they thought it an unnecessary subject, and what was worse, they were treated like children at those lectures and weren't going to stand for it.

He went on to complain about the low standard of literature in Russia today. A theme like war had produced good novels and plays, but nowadays there was a dearth of conflict in Russia. The present Soviet system could not give poets the material they needed, he added—with something of an ironic smile. It seemed to me a poor outlook for future Russian literary effort as all traces of conflict are gradually erased from Communist society. What will there be left for the creative writers of the future?

Today I also had my first "tutorial" with Pustavoyt. We discussed Turgenev's *Fathers and Sons*, of which I had unfortunately only had time to read half. He explained the background of the novel, and emphasised strongly the difference between the Liberals—from the upper classes, of the Bazarov type—and the Nihilists—the Revolutionary Radical. After we had agreed that human beings had to have some principles to live by, he tried to show that in fact Bazarov had principles too, but they did not come to anything, because Bazarov saw it as his

The house of Leo Tolstoi at Yasnaya Poly-ana, which Sej-ersted visited. Right: Tolstoi's grave lies be-neath trees on his estate.

main duty simply to promote liberal doctrines which amounted only to empty talk.

I remarked that Bazarov was in no sense a practical man, and that he himself only embodied empty talk. Pustavoyt agreed. He said in view of Turgenev's background this was bound to be so, for he himself belonged to the category of "mere liberals". One could, however, find *positive* types of the same class as Bazarov in the works of genuine radical authors, like Tchernichevchy.

In the evening an architectural student visited us to look at a book containing pictures of Norwegian houses, which Ingjald had with him. It would have been pleasant if his visit had not been so protracted.

Monday, February 22

Today was the first really good day we've had. Ingjald and I made our way over the hills towards the river. There we encountered a mass of humanity and lots of skiers—and we took dozens of pictures. When it came to lunch we found that both the better-class restaurants were closed.

It's just impossible to keep track of all these openings and closings, and furthermore at any time restaurants seem likely to have their "hygiene days". If by chance one should descend upon a restaurant that happens not to be serving food at the time, one is speedily made aware of the fact by a group of waitresses standing in the doorway shouting "sakryt!" (closed) in a very objectionable fashion. This is only one of the many examples of a complete lack of service encountered everywhere. Despite the fact that Russians can be extremely charming, they have absolutely no conception of serving people. I wonder if, in attempting theoretically to eradicate social distinctions, they haven't confused service with servility?

Yesterday we hung on the walls of our rooms some Norwegian tourist posters which Ingjald had brought. That cheered things up a bit. On the whole the room is decent enough—small, but light, attractive and well decorated. Ingjald and I share the entrance hall, the shower and the lavatory. Unfortunately, there was no warm water to be had from the shower this morning.

Today we were sorry to learn that we would be having a newcomer at our Language Institute—hitherto there has only been Ingjald and myself. The other news is that everything is being got ready for the Chekhov Centenary. Madame Rassodova has promised to get us tickets for *The Cherry Tree*, as well as for an excursion to various places connected with Chekhov in Moscow.

Tuesday, February 23

At today's lecture I talked to Peter again. He told me he had a bad leg and must go to hospital for a week or more. We had previously agreed to go to a theatre together, but he was sorry this would not be possible now. I cannot wholly escape the suspicion that there have perhaps been other reasons than his leg for his absence from the lectures, and his crying off from the theatre. We must see whether he turns up again . . .

After language instruction I went to a seminar on Russian Realism, held by Professor Bondi. The auditorium was full, with a more mixed and colourful gathering than at lectures I had previously attended. This is in no sense an obligatory lecture; but I was told that the professor was one of the most popular in the Faculty. He also proved to be a very charming man, but spoke with so little clarity that I didn't get much benefit. He began by expounding what realism was. Unless I am mistaken, he declared that realism must be popular, and must also be artistic—and if it was popular, it was automatically artistic and realistic. Similarly, if it was to be artistic, it must also be realistic and popular! Perhaps I have not done him justice; but he certainly established an identity between art and realistic art.

He also discussed art appreciation, and insisted that all understanding of art must be subjective, based on a man's own feelings and opinions.

Thursday, February 25

A strong Norwegian delegation recently came to Moscow to negotiate the building of power stations on the Pasvik River, which marks the frontier between North Norway and the Soviet Union. My next-door neighbour in Oslo was one of them, so yesterday I went to see him at the Hotel Ukraine. As a result I missed question time, but the lady teacher was very understanding. Furthermore, she praised me yesterday for my work which is always encouraging. On the whole I feel that my progress with Russian is somewhat erratic; sometimes I am pleased and at other times dissatisfied.

Last night we were invited out by some of the American exchange scholarship students, and were given popcorn. There are about 25 Americans here, all of them agreeable and intelligent—first class representatives of the Western world.

Sunday, February 28

On Thursday evening a lecture was organised in the recreation room on our floor. An elderly woman lecturer talked about "Two months in the U.S.A". She had actually visited American universities and the content of her talk—as might have been expected—overemphasised the negative aspects, and made endless comparisons in favour of the Soviet Union.

On the subject of the standard of living, for example, her main point was that this increased at a faster rate in the Soviet Union than in the USA. "and that is true progress". (This complex-ridden attitude, forever on the defensive, and the desire to seize every opportunity of showing how perfect one is, seems all too typical a tendency in Russia—it is certainly very tedious. At the same time it can undoubtedly be regarded as a sign of inward weakness).

Some of the American students present were naturally irritated, and began to interject questions and supplementary information, so that by the end things got quite lively, with more and more of the audience joining in. The lecturer eventually flung out the remark that the Americans whom she had met in the USA were somewhat politer and friendlier than those present. When a Soviet student asked whether she could not also say a little about what she had *liked* in America, she began to speak of the beauties of nature!

Afterwards, each of the Western representatives found himself surrounded by a group of Russians eager to discuss matters. As a result we had a five-hours' debate on everything from capitalism to Hungary but nothing really noteworthy was said. Unearned income was one of the main themes—which was easy enough to deal with, since there are people in Russia today drawing unearned incomes! The Public Savings Bank in fact offers three per cent interest: and once it was admitted that millionaires were to be found in Russia, it was easy enough to realise that some of these must be able to do very well on their "unearned income".

Of course, the answer to this was that in a capitalist society money entails power; but on this their ideas were between 50 and 100 years out of date.

As for the party system, they could not understand. If everybody wanted what was best for the nation, they argued, then all parties must end up with the same programmes, so there appeared to be no need for more than one party in a genuinely democratic country!

On Hungary, I found them disappointingly ready to defend the Soviet Government's action. The debate culminated in their producing a Hungarian student who said he had been in Budapest at the time of the uprising. He talked about the Fascists and criminals who had allegedly been behind it, and the American weapons that had been sent to Budapest in Red Cross cars. Finally, I pointed out that in Norway I knew a number of Hungarian students who had taken part in the fighting in Budapest and who had given quite a different version. I had thus had the benefit of first hand information from both sides, and was in a position to judge more objectively than those who had heard only one side of the story.

One Soviet student declared that I must be naive to suppose that that could furnish a basis of objectivity: evidently "objectivity" means something different in the Soviet Union from what it means in the West. In general they use a quite peculiar terminology, which gives one the feeling, in discussion with them, of beating one's head against the wall. The argument I found most convincing was that no one, and certainly not the Hungarians, would wish to have foreign troops on their own soil—surely the Russians could understand that!

The debate bore witness to a one-sided outlook that was discouraging. There are, however, two factors that should not be overlooked. First, we all have a tendency to put the best construction on our own side's behaviour, if it is subjected to outside attack. Russians usually have a strong national pride which fortifies this tendency. Secondly, we only spoke to a group of students, of whom, moreover, a small minority took an active part in the discussion. One does not know what the silent listeners thought.

On Friday I joined an excursion to the Chekhov memorials in Moscow. My main impression was of the dreadful cold! In the evening I was visited by a "Sanitary Commission", consisting of three students who looked for dust in the most incredible places—and found it. As a result, I was given only "Third Character" for cleanliness in my room . . . and this has now been written up outside in the corridor. A striking example of what "collective living" means in practice—one's private life becomes a public affair.

On Saturday we had another talk on Hertzen, and afterwards I went to an exhibition of paintings glorifying the Revolution. In the evening I saw *Prince Igor* at the Bolshoi. Quite impressive; in line with the Soviet sense for effect, both live horses and real fire were used on the stage.

Today (Sunday) I went out with the Norwegian delegation to Zagorsk, some 70 km. north of Moscow, to see the Monastery. I acted as interpreter to the group. The Monastery is of course something of an ecclesiastical centre, containing among other things, a Higher Institute of Theology. We attended a mass, at which a large number of people were present, most of them admittedly old women.

In the afternoon I was visited by a Russian student named Albert, who had taken part in the earlier discussion. He had put a couple of questions but otherwise played only a passive role. He asked if Ingjald and I would like to come up to his room to hear some music. This turned out to be American jazz, of an ancient vintage. We talked a bit about art, and decided to go together to the Tretyakov Gallery on Sunday.

Albert is 21, and is doing the Second Course in the Faculty of Physics. He said that in the summer he works on the land. For a year before he started at the University, he worked as a plumber and coal heaver. He told us that summer work was not compulsory for the students, nor was it in any way necessary for his particular studies. I asked whether, in accordance with the new school regula- tions, it was not necessary to work for a time before going to University, but he said he didn't think so.

We also discussed language teaching in schools.

This, he said, began for Russian children at the age of five. Most children learned English, many also learned French and German, though not more than one language. Despite the fact that a child could thus have six years at one language, Albert did not think many children knew very much when they left school. My own experience is that one rarely meets a Soviet student with whom one can converse in any other language than Russian.

Finally, we talked about literature. His favourite writer was Leonide Andreyev. He appeared somewhat indifferent about Dostoievsky, and he would not discuss the Pasternak case, since he had not read *Dr. Zhivago* (banned in Russia anyway).

LIFE ON THE LENIN HILLS

Tuesday, March 1

The *starrosta* on our floor—which is the name given to a student entrusted with various practical and administrative duties—is an older student called Jakobson. He has just come in to say that the door absolutely must be locked when one leaves the room—there have been cases of theft on our floor.

This is all slightly comic when one realises that the keys to all doors are the same !

At the Language Institute yesterday I heard that the American students had been refused permission to hold an exhibition which they had prepared. This dealt with a subject chosen from American cultural life—and they had chosen the American educational system. Everything was ready when they were told the subject was unacceptable.

Yesterday the new student joined our group, an East German, a red-blooded Communist but otherwise quite pleasant.

In the evening Jakobson came in again, this time to inform me that the light must be turned off when one leaves the room. The reason, he gave jokingly, was that full Communism had not yet been attained in the electricity supply ! We invited him to come in and sit down and he remained until 2.30 in the morning telling us his life story.

His father, a high-ranking soldier, had been executed in the Moscow trials when Jakobson was only 14. Many people had lived in terror at that time—consequently he had not a good word to say about Stalin.   Since then Jakobson had fought in the war, including the Battles of Stalingrad and Berlin.   In 1945 he had been demobilised as Section Commander, and had then begun working in the mines of Sakhalin. Five years later he moved to Tomsk, where he worked as a kind of Youth Leader, doing his matriculation on the side. Now he was in his last year in the Physics Faculty at Moscow University.

He talked openly and intelligently on the shortcomings of Soviet society today. As his background showed, he had seen and experienced a good deal, and seemed to know what he was talking about. He said there was much corruption, certainly more than in Norway. Above all, people were generally lazy. Many workers in the collective farms, for example, were only concerned to cultivate their own little patch of ground and to drink vodka. If one visited the new cultivation areas in the south, one could see that the farmers who ought to have been working merely lay around and "spat and drank vodka", while it was groups of students (among others) who did the actual work. Apart from that, there was a very agreeable atmosphere in these newly cultivated districts, so if the idea appealed to us we ought to try and visit them—though he expressed some doubt as to whether we would get permission.

Jakobson bewailed the manner in which people believed everything they read in the papers, as in Stalin's day. He implied that there was now more basis for such belief: but he did allow himself the mild observation that only one side of the story got printed.

He was a very nice chap, and up to a point intelligent. But for all his intelligence he had an unquenchable—and for me, touchingly naive— faith in the "thousand years' *Reich*".

"In 60 to 100 years", he said, "when we have achieved our material aims, everyone will be good and kind like Lenin. Then we shall have no more collective farms, only State farms" (not *kolkhoz*, but *sovkhoz*"). I expressed my cautious and decadent doubts!

In many ways Jakobson's type is impressive. It is an achievement to retain one's idealism after going through all he had experienced, and after acquiring so objective an outlook.

Sunday, March 6

The last week has been incredibly busy. Something has happened every day. On Tuesday evening we visited a Danish girl student, together with some Embassy officials, an American and a Sudanese. On Wednesday evening a few Americans came in and we drank pepper-vodka. On Thursday at noon we went to a dress rehearsal for a new ballet at the Bolshoi: *The Hump-Backed Ass*. We had been given free tickets by Madame Rassodova.

Afterwards I had a talk with Pustavoyt, who had been requested by the Foreign Bureau to draw up a plan for my literary studies. We agreed that I should read, and discuss weekly with him, certain works of Tolstoy, Dostoievsky, Turgenev and Chekhov. His own original proposal for fortnightly tutorials, which had suited both of us so well, was now superseded. Undoubtedly the Foreign Bureau is behind the new proposal. I took the precaution of pointing out to him that I was not here primarily to read books that I could equally well read at home, and could not guarantee that I could get through all the works he had prescribed. He took my point. I got the impression that the essential thing was to draw up in writing something that the Foreign Bureau would regard as satisfactory. In addition, it was agreed that I should attend twice weekly his lectures on the "Golden Age".

On Thursday afternoon Albert came along with two friends for a talk. He was interested in knowing what sort of information about the Soviet Union would be obtained in the West. I replied that a mass of information was available from all quarters and that it was up to us to assess its value. He said he had the feeling that the Americans had a one-sided picture; they were capable of asking quite puerile questions about the Soviet Union. I admitted this could be so, but added that questions asked by Soviet students were sometimes even more childish, and that their picture of the West was still more one-sided. He did not deny this, but said it was necessary to keep out all Western capitalist propaganda that might do harm. Then he suggested it would be better

The centre of Soviet indoctrination, Moscow University stands on Lenin Hills. The main 32-storey building is the tallest in Europe and it has a total of 45,000 rooms.

to drop the argument, which might impair our friendship.

On Friday I bought a *chapka* (a fur hat) for 100 roubles—it is large and black. Ingjald and I went to lunch with the Norwegian Ambassador.

At Saturday's lecture Peter reappeared, his leg evidently improved, and I had a few words with him. He said three members of his course had recently been expelled from the University—one of them because he had not managed to keep up with the course, the other two for "different reasons". In the interval, the lady inspector for the course again mounted the rostrum, to scold—by name—a couple of students who had dodged some lectures.

In the evening I met one of my friends from our recent discussion group, called Yuri. I had promised to look him up some time—he lived on the floor above in a room with two others. When I arrived, they were preparing to celebrate the 19th birthday of one of his friends, and I was promptly invited. Yuri was in his second year at the Faculty of Physics. He was clearly a member of the party, which is rather rare among students. Before coming to the University, he had served for three years in the army, ending up as a sergeant of the top grade. He was a strong, healthy, cheerful type—the sort that seems to come out on top in all circumstances.

We talked about ideology in general terms. I emphasised that there were a number of different ideological tendencies in the West, and that we were free to choose among them. He replied that people made such curious choices sometimes, that it was better for them to be shown the way. Naturally, parents had the right to bring up their children— just as a people had to be educated and protected from bad influences. (One could hardly imagine a

49

more forthright expression of the patriarchal attitude. This is typical of Russia, both before and since the Revolution, and makes such a strange impression on Westerners). After a time the discussion was interrupted by the arrival of other guests, in festive mood.

The party was a jolly one. We ate and drank a lot, toasting peace and friendship. I explained in advance that if I did not drain my glass in one go (which was the habit), it was not because I was opposed to peace and friendship! Afterwards we had singing and recitation . . . and then we danced. One of my partners was a charming little girl with the attractive name of Nonna.

Today (Sunday) we went to the crowded Tretyakov Gallery with Albert. As foreigners we were allowed to by-pass a long queue. In the evening I went to a performance of *The Cherry Orchard*. Madame Rossodova and her husband were also there. I greeted her and her husband remarked that he had heard of my love for Dostoievsky, which he could not understand, since he considered Dostoievsky a very poor novelist. At this point his wife interrupted, suggesting we should talk about something else—if we continued to discuss Dostoievsky there would only be a violent argument.

Thursday, March 10

The Norwegian-speaking Sacha came to see us on Monday. He wanted our help in translating some *risqué* stories by Nils Johan Rud, which we gave him.

Tuesday was the so-called International Women's Day, and the newspapers were full of it. Evidently it is a real holiday here in Russia. Both the best restaurants at the University were closed, as always happens when there is anything special going on. There was also a great deal of noise in the corridors at night.

At the lecture I was attending, both the teacher and the inspectress expressed their best wishes for the occasion to all the girls present. The inspectress wished them happiness in their private lives, success in their studies, but above all that they should become good Soviet citizens. In return, she was given some dried up bouquets of flowers by one of the students (fresh flowers are very hard to get).

On Wednesday evening we had a big discussion on our floor about philosophical problems to do with art. I was there most of the time, but unfortunately did not understand everything that was said. There was of course an official know-all to express the "correct" opinion, but he encountered some strong opposition. It is evident that people think and express themselves more freely on art than about politics, here. The interest in art is also very keen and there were many enthusiastic participants in the discussion. From time to time, Mr. Know-all intervened, to make a correction, or to gloss over something that had been said. He spoke of Communism as the obvious purpose of art, and of artists' subordination to it. The educational significance of art was also much in evidence.

He was interrupted by one student who wanted to establish the general principles of art—not only for socialist art, but for the art that had always existed in every kind of society, including primitive and capitalist societies. He himself considered that these principles consisted of art's function as a means of expressing thoughts and feelings that could not be expressed in any other way. Seen thus, art was a form of perception.

Against him it was argued that art should always demonstrate what was best, and progressive, in life and in society. As an example that even Turgenev had erred in this respect, Mr. Know-all referred to Turgenev's Russian women peasants—pathetic, poetical figures who almost exceeded the bounds of reality. The right attitude was that of Tchernichevsky, who depicted strong, healthy women. Here someone broke in to ask, amid laughter: "Are only the strong and healthy worth writing about?" Later there were frequent concessions that "bourgeois" artists, too, could create good art, so there must be some yard-stick for art other than its moral and progressive subject matter.

During one eloquent intervention by Mr. Know-all, someone behind me whispered "All this is just words". Another speaker, in talking about the moral content of art, used the expression "the so-called Communist morality". When he immediately corrected this to "No, not so-called—*the Communist morality*", there was mild laughter.

Sunday March 13

On Thursday I had my last tutorial on *Fathers and Sons*. Pustavoyt sought to establish, on the basis of the book's last chapter, that Turgenev was fundamentally a pessimist. I tried to argue that one could equally read in this an optimistic faith in the lasting power of love. He immediately agreed with me! On the whole, I have the impression that he is not at all concerned to indoctrinate me, and is surprisingly ready to agree with my opinions.

On Friday, there was the first whiff of spring in the air. Albert came in for a while, and I asked him about the possibility of skiing on Sunday. He said he would ask some of his friends to come along, to show me where the ski slopes were.

At Saturday's lecture, Peter and I agreed to go to an art exhibition next week. He also asked me about literary criticism in Norway, and mentioned that people were tentative and unsure in this field in the Soviet Union.

In the evening I saw Moyseyf's Dance Company at the Tchaikowsky Hall, and was very impressed.

This morning Albert's friend Pavel came along to take Ingjald and me skiing. I had brought my own skis from Norway, but we had some difficulty in finding a pair for Ingjald. We took the metro down town, and then a train from the Leningrad station to a small place called Podreskovo, just outside Chimski. This was as far as we were in fact allowed to travel outside Moscow, but we met no sort of control. The ski ground itself, the surface of the snow and the weather were all excellent.

Wednesday, March 16

I went to the GUM Store on Monday to buy a *chapka* for a friend in France who had asked me to send him one. I managed to get quite a cheap one for 57 roubles, and I asked the assistant if it would be possible to send it to France. She replied yes.

It proved to be quite the reverse. How typical ! Everything one asks about is said to be possible.

One can write what one likes in the newspapers, one can travel where ever one wishes, and one can send *chapkas* abroad. Words and facts just do not correspond. If anything at all is to be read into these assurances, it can only be that everything will be possible in the course of the "thousand years' *Reich*"!

I went all over the place with my *chapka*. At the first post office I was told that only souvenirs could be sent abroad, and that a *chapka* could not be regarded as a souvenir. I was directed to the main post office, where I argued my way past a number of people to an inspector. According to him, it was quite impossible to send any fur article abroad. Presumably these are all needed in Russia, because it is so cold.

In the evening I went to the Friendship House again, for the return of the Olympic Team. The Institute had given me a ticket.

Last Thursday our lecturer began to talk about Turgenev. Peter turned up and cried off the art exhibition we were to have visited in the afternoon, because the whole of his course had to take part in a Komsomol meeting. I asked at once if I could also attend. He hesitated, then asked whether I was a Communist (odd that he had not realised long ago that I could not possibly be !), but ended by asking permission from the Komsomol leader, who granted it.

Shortly before the meeting Peter told me that about 90 per cent of the students were members of the Komsomol but only a small minority (about three per cent) belonged to the party. It was a great honour to be admitted into the party. The Komsomol boss, Victor, who conducted the meeting, was one of the lucky ones. There were only two or three mammoth gatherings for the whole course each term. They were usually very lively and entertaining, with keen discussion. On this occasion two points were on the agenda. One entailed a discussion on the behaviour of two students who were named. Peter observed that this was *pour encourager les autres*, and told me the whole story. Earlier in the term, the two students had deliberately left the course to become ordinary labourers in Baku, the reason being apparently that they wanted (so they said) "to see life at first hand". This sounded to me like a typical bit of Communist window-dressing. The object of the discussion was to establish whether they had acted correctly or not. The second item was the wall-sheet published by the course, which had not been giving satisfaction recently.

The discussion was genuinely a live one. Someone got up and said that he had known personally the two students, Valeri and Theodore, but he found it difficult to explain why they acted as they had. However, if people cared to ask him concrete questions he would do his best to answer them.

Voice from the hall: "What reasons had they for leaving?"

The speaker declared that he had put that question to them, but Valeri had simply answered, in the most blue-eyed way, that he should wait and see (laughter!) Clearly they had a genuine desire to experience life at first hand. Valeri was a natural artist, and must live in order to be able to create. As for Theodore, the explanation was probably that he was under Valeri's influence.

Victor, the boss, then got up and said that he had also spoken to the two students before their departure. Valeri said he did not get much out of the university; life there was not interesting enough.

Here of course the boss could not agree: it was a mistake to find life at the university not interesting.

Another speaker said that Valeri's sole ambition was to write poetry. This had been the case when he first came to the university, and it was the reason for his leaving it. His mistake was that he had not participated enough in the University's communal life. If he had done so he would have found life more interesting.

One of the women bosses criticised Valeri's claim that he had wanted to see life in order to write about it. Life was everywhere. If he could not find it in one place, he was no more likely to find it in another. The trouble lay in Valeri himself.

Peter spoke next, and also criticised Valeri, whom he described as a type of the 1920s. We live in a new epoch, he said, in which society needed above all educated people. Valeri was a Don Quixote, who ignored reality.

Then came a feeble defence of Valeri. Perhaps he was naive, but there was something infinitely good in him, which deserved respect. He was bursting with ambitions—he wanted to cook, to lead, everything! Furthermore, he had been a good member of the Komsomol. (Theodore did not seem to merit so much consideration).

A graceful little number then stood up to put the view that Valeri was honest and good. He did not believe in the existence of bad people, she said, and he had done the right thing.

This sentiment was soon swamped in a blistering attack by an older, more determined and quite eloquent type. There were considerable weaknesses in the actions of the two students, he said. They had been unable to adjust themselves to the collective in which they lived. Consequently they ran away from it instead of fighting, within the collective, to orientate themselves. Furthermore, in a centre of culture like Moscow one had a better opportunity to learn about life and culture than anywhere else.

Then it was the turn of the wall journal to come under fire. This was alleged to have been so awful that the editor had been sacked. To general consternation the sacked editor stood up and declared that a wall newspaper was unnecessary, anyway. It had been proved, he said, by the fact that generally he had received no contributions during the whole of his editorship. He sat out the ensuing debate with an expression both sour and fed up.

Several students protested: "But we *must* have a wall newspaper". This represented the outward side of student life at the University and in it one should be able to write about life among students—not clip bits from elsewhere, as the ex-editor had done.

Voice from the back: "Is life among us so interesting, then . . . ?"

The argument went backwards and forwards like a shuttlecock, and finished with no decision being reached.

This was the Komsomol . . . having a session of self-criticism.

Saturday, March 19

On Thursday evening Ingjald and I were invited out again by the Norwegian delegation.

Yesterday I spring-cleaned my room. And only just in time, too. For in the afternoon the "sanitary commission" turned up—the most pettifogging one so far. For the lavatory and shower-room they gave us a dressing down, and I collected two marks.

Today, however, Jakobson called in and explained in a very friendly way how and where we could get hold of a brush and bucket. So we'll have to get to work on that shower-room.

Monday, March 21

I am beginning to get into the rhythm of things. Time goes quickly. Today I received three letters from home—exactly as last Monday. It looks as though the Norwegian Section of the Censor's Office has a part-time job ! Actually, I can find no evidence that my letters are being tampered with. It could be that they have only a weekly delivery.

On Sunday I was out on skis along the whole of the Lenin Hills. The weather and the snow tell of spring. Later one of the Americans came in and we chatted for a while.

Yesterday I was invited by Nonna, the Russian student of physics, to a concert. She brought along her friend Tamara. I entertained the girls for a long time by telling them of student life in Norway, how one could arrange one's time as one wished, and how one could get scholarships to travel all over the place. They seemed interested. Quite obviously they were not used to hearing this sort of thing. It was like a different world to them.

Friday, March 25

There was a Chekhov evening at the Institute on Tuesday. It began with a lecture, after which students from various countries made brief contributions. Karl Kramer spoke very well as the American representative. A small Chinese girl also showed herself skilful in adapting her contribution to Communist propaganda. Some young actors then did short scenes from Chekhov, and finally we had a quiz competition.

On Wednesday I saw the film *White Nights*, an adaptation of Dostoievsky's novel. I thought it was good and genuinely Dostoievskian. Official Russian opinion is not, however, happy about it. It is considered too sentimental. There may be some truth in this, but the story itself is after all not free from sentimentality.

I was not too well prepared for Thursday's tutorial, and Pustavoyt was clearly dissatisfied, particularly at the fact that I could not memorise a passage from one of Turgenev's stories which Lenin had regarded very highly. The story concerned a land-owner who wanted his servant beaten up because he had not produced the wine at the right temperature.

Afterwards I noticed in the corridor outside a board on which had been written up the results and descriptions of the activities of various courses, e.g. agitation, cleanliness in students' rooms, and actual studies. Evidently there was a measure of competition between the various courses in the Faculty. Under the heading "Komsomol Meetings" was a reference to the meeting I had attended. There had been a good discussion, it said, but it was regrettable that some of the contributions had consisted of personal attacks on the two students whose behaviour had been the subject of debate. Three people were named in this connection, one of them Peter. . . .

On Friday there was a formal opening of an exhibition at the Pushkin Museum of drawings by Munch, a well known Norwegian artist of the early 20th century. It seems odd that a proper exhibition of paintings could not have been sent over when the opportunity offered. Their effect, amid so much dreary Soviet art, would have been miraculous.

Monday, March 28

At the lecture I suggested to Peter Veselov that we should visit the Munch exhibition. Peter seemed interested. He told me, incidentally, that he never attended more than five lectures a week. This was less than half the obligatory number, but nobody took it seriously. He also mentioned that on the following day the whole of his year were going out on a building job. This was compulsory, and they were expected to do four working Sundays a year. I asked him if he would be going on the job. Peter replied that he had organised a doctor's certificate for himself, claiming there was something wrong with his leg, so he wouldn't have to go.

I heard another student complaining: "This work is supposed to be educative, but we're being educated all the time and we get sick of it".

On Saturday evening Albert called in, and I tried to explain to him the relationship between a director and a workman. I also happened to mention at some point in the talk that I was a Conservative. He nearly laughed himself to death. I don't think he'd ever set eyes on a Conservative before.

On Sunday I visited the new building area south of the University. Enormous but tedious buildings.

The only exception was the new Chinese Embassy—a fine modern building among some rather outmoded architecture.

In the evening I was invited by a fellow Russian student, Alexander, to a concert. It was beautifully given by a French quartet which took five curtain calls.

Alexander is very nice but seems a little immature. We talked politics in general terms. He said he had heard that there was little difference between the two United States political parties, the Republicans and the Democrats, and thought it a bit unnecessary to have two parties. I explained as best I could the principles of the multi-party system, and I think he understood enough of it. But he thought the Soviet system worked very well. I pointed out to him the inherent possibilities of a misuse of power in such a system, and cited Stalin as an example of how this had already happened (one should always play on their weak points to get anywhere in a discussion, we discovered).

He agreed that Stalin had acted badly in some ways, but declared that by and large he had been a great man, particularly as a Marxist theoretician.

And anyway, said Alexander, people in the West did not understand what Communism was. Their ideas about the Soviet Union were completely crazy. They only knew what Western propaganda told them.

I played an old record by replying that as far as I could see the people of the Soviet Union had an even crazier opinion of the West. Alexander said quite politely that it seemed we were all satisfied with our own systems of government.

Then we got onto the subject of the meaning of liberty, and I put forward the view that in all probability the Soviets and the Western world had

61

different interpretations of this term. Alexander replied that he was unable to understand the Western interpretation of liberty, so I offered some small, simplified but concrete examples. I said that if an artist, for example, was a Christian and wished to express his belief through his art, and if there were people who were interested in these works of art, then this had nothing whatever to do with the State. His beliefs and his means of expressing them were his own affair. Alexander replied with a laugh that he couldn't understand how intelligent people could be Christians. I said simply that there were many intelligent people who were Christians. "I'm astonished", Alexander said.

Alexander is a second year physics student. He told me that physics students who took a degree from the University did not get jobs as teachers, but went into laboratories and institutes. He had about eight or nine compulsory lectures a week plus two two-hour periods of gymnastics. These were only compulsory for the first two years. I asked him if the work was hard. That depended on the student, he replied. Alexander said he hadn't the patience to study all that much. Students had to sit for examinations at the end of each term. In addition to physics and allied subjects they had to study English and Russian—and during the first two years, the history of the Communist Party. They also had philosophy. When I asked if this meant only Marxism-Leninism, Alexander smiled. "That's more or less the case", he said.

"THEY CAN'T WIN"

Sunday, April 3

On Monday I had a visit from two Western students. We drank Norwegian aquavit and swapped experiences. They told me about a Russian student who had said that people in the Soviet Union often toyed with the idea that one day in the future it may be necessary for the Soviet Union and the USA to join forces again to defeat Germany. My friends had then told him that Westerners often imagined that the Soviet Union and the USA might have to join forces one day to defend themselves against China. This idea had been very surprising and completely new to the Russians.

On Tuesday afternoon Albert popped in for a chat, and once again we got round to discussing whether one had the right to choose one's own ideology. I tried in my bad Russian to explain my own concept of freedom. Albert said he had given a good deal of thought to the subject, and even if he could not accept my point of view, he was nevertheless remarkably mild in his reasoning—and fairly objective. He said he fully realised that it was impossible to prove that one ideology was absolutely right in relation to certain subjectively chosen aims. I thought at this point I might even get him to condemn the totalitarian system under which he was living, but he didn't.

When we got on to the concept of God, he produced almost an agnostic point of view, rather than directly atheistic (which is by no means unimportant, even if at the same time he said he believed in the millenium). He did not think it could be scientifically proved that God existed, yet equally it could not be

A Whit-Sunday scene outside the cathedral in Vladimir. The crowd cannot get in because it is already packed. Below: Modern Russia has not lost its beggars. They line up for alms in Vladimir.

proved that God doesn't exist, which I thou[g]
a little spiritual concession and certainly ou[t]
with Communist atheistic dogma, in spite o[f]
professed "scientific" props.

I think Albert is probably a very typical Soviet
student, or at least typical of a certain category.
Behind the facade he has an independent mind. But
as he was not born to be a martyr, and as he may
allow himself unconsciously to be influenced by the
pressure all round him, his mind will not react
against the conditions under which he lives.

Curiously enough, Albert himself drew attention
to this subjective influence on individual opinions
under pressure from outside circumstances. He
realised that this phenomenon existed in Russia, but
referred to Norwegian Communists as a worse
example. Albert thought they could hardly be good
Communists since they were so much under the
influence of a capitalist society. Probably they were
infiltrated by capitalist and imperialist opinions. I
replied that Norwegian Communists were "purer"
than any others.

Albert pressed home his conviction that the
difficulties of being in opposition to one's society
were insurmountable.

His point that it must be difficult to be a Communist in Norway leads me only to the reflection
that Albert is a perfect example of how difficult it
would be to be a capitalist in Russia.

Peter came in after Albert had gone. I showed him
the few art books we had and he was very interested.
The sketch which made the deepest impression on
him was one of a soldier—shot and hanging over
barbed wire. Above his head shone the rays of a
crucifix with the body of Christ hanging in the same
way. With typical Russian feeling for drama and

xpression, he sat for a long time in silent admiration of this picture.

I walked with him to the lift and bumped into Yuri, Alexander, and a few others. Though I tried to avoid it, we were soon back on the subject of the meaning of liberty once more. And to my surprise, after a lot of talk, the group agreed that freedom of speech did not exist in the Soviet Union. (One learns little by little which ploys to use in order to get under the students' guard. One can, for example, press them on terminology and it usually turns out that they are simply using a collection of propaganda phrases. Nonetheless, it must be pretty rare to hear a group of Soviet students admit that there is no freedom of speech in the USSR).

To counterbalance this startling confession, they went on that freedom of speech was but a very small part of liberty. Real freedom, they said, was economic, in that employment was absolutely assured, etc. It seemed rather as though some of them thought economic freedom ruled out freedom of speech.

One student also aired the opinion that the liberty of the individual was not so important as that of the State. I tried in vain to get him to explain what he meant by the "liberty of the State". I assume that either this was just a meaningless phrase—which I suspect was the case—or that my basic beliefs will not permit me to understand this concept.

During the discussion Yuri said, rather significantly, that all of us from the West seemed to have our own individual way of discussing and defending our ideas, whereas all the Soviet students appeared to have more or less identical opinions and arguments. I pounced on this heaven-sent opening to explain why I thought Yuri's observations were perfectly correct.

The evening closed with a description by an older student of how four Russian soldiers had recently survived for 40 days on a raft in the Pacific. He said quite seriously that they had only managed to survive because of their mental calibre. They had been equipped with this strength through being Soviet citizens, nurtured collectively by the State and shaped into healthy human beings. Had they been Americans, he added cynically, they would undoubtedly have eaten each other after ten days or so.

Surprisingly, while we were having our general debate one of the Russians tried several times to support my point of view, but he was pretty sharply attacked by the others.

On Tuesday I visited a big art exhibition. It seemed flat and negative—lots of sunburned tractor drivers and building workers in heroic toiling poses, and innumerable busts of Lenin staring into the future. But there were several very charming things in the applied arts section. Nonetheless it was pointed out to me that you couldn't buy any of these things in the shops.

On Thursday I saw Pustavoyt again. I feel that he is becoming increasingly uninterested in me.

The feeling is mutual.

During the afternoon a student from Uganda dropped in and we talked for quite a time. He was studying medicine in Moscow—apparently at the expense of the Soviet Union. It is fantastic what tremendous efforts the Soviets make to conquer the less-developed countries. But they had certainly backed a loser in my friend from Uganda. He was very pro-Western and crammed with anti-Communist opinions.

I got him to give me his views about the new People's Friendship University for coloured students which is due to open later this year. He said it was a particularly clumsy piece of discrimination to set up a special university for coloured people.

He told me he had studied for two years at London University, where there were a couple of thousand coloured students. Nobody there had ever considered weeding them out into a university of their own.

He added that he had mentioned all this to an interviewer from the University newspaper—but that naturally nothing had appeared in print. He also said that recently there had been several cases of racial persecution at Moscow University.

One African had been beaten up by three Russian students because he had danced with a Russian girl. It had also been decreed by the University Party Committee that Russian girl students were forbidden to visit coloured students in their rooms, or to invite them to their own rooms.

(I've since heard that the term "coloured" students also embraces Arabs. The background to this decree is believed to be the allegation that a contingent of Arab students who were here last year left behind an amazing number of illegitimate children!)

Alongside these views of coloured students in the Soviet Union, I should mention a conversation I overheard in the restaurant between a Russian and a Syrian student. The Syrian who spoke very bad Russian said he was a Socialist and praised President Nasser to the skies. But he emphasised that he was not what the Russians would call a Socialist. In his country one could, for example, own many things— even one's own business. The only thing one couldn't own were the big factories. Furthermore, he said, the standard of living was much higher than in the Soviet Union. He mentioned that his main subject was philosophy and that he was in the Soviet Union for the purpose of studying materialism. In a very fatherly manner he went on to say that it was impossible to study any other aspects of philosophy in Russia. The Russian student was obviously astonished and said that one could study *everything* in Moscow.

The Syrian wouldn't have it . . .

On Friday I went along with Peter to the Munch Exhibition. He was most interested and I did my best to explain things to him. When I spoke of Munch's life and his melancholia, Peter referred to the problem of insanity in the Soviet Union. He said it was a very great problem. He knew of some university professors who had either been or still were in lunatic asylums or nerve sanatoria. He knew something about it because there had been insanity in his own family. His eldest brother, an engineer, who had become a director of a factory at an early age, had a mental breakdown and had to be sent to an asylum. He was now at home with his mother but was incapable of doing any work.

Today, Sunday, Alexander came in for a while. I tried, with the help of statistics, to give him a picture of the standard of living and social work in Norway.

Friday, April 8

By and large it's been a good week. On Tuesday my Russian friend who'd tried to defend me earlier came in again to have a look at some American magazines I had. Then Albert turned up. He,

Ingjald and I discussed the objectivity or otherwise of the information available in the Soviet Union, particularly on West Germany.

We became very tired of edging our way through the discussion. Finally Ingjald could stand the prevarication no longer. He almost blew up and said straight out that Soviet propaganda lied. Albert's immediate reaction was to withdraw to his defensive position, but despite everything I think it is good to have a flare-up now and again to clear the air.

On Thursday evening Alexander came in and announced that it was his birthday. He proposed to organise a little party and wanted Ingjald and me to go along. We said we'd be delighted to go—and forgot we had asked Sasha to drop in.

At the party there were about 15 people from Alexander's group at the Faculty of Physics. We ate and drank and Alexander was given a guitar by his pals. The fellow sitting next to me said there were about 4,500 students in the Faculty of Physics itself, and about 500 students in each year. Contrary to what Albert had told me, he said that all students had to do building or other work for at least one month every summer. Work in the new cultivation areas, however, was voluntary and could be done instead of the compulsory labour.

Monday, April 11

On Saturday, after the lecture, Peter told me that his group was going to have a discussion on the teachings of Lenin. They had these discussions frequently, he said. Usually the group selected its own theme but on this occasion the woman teacher

A Russian woman crosses herself at a Moscow church. Below: members of a Norwegian delegation meet a priest in Zagorsk.

had chosen. I immediately asked if I could go along and Peter later inquired. The teacher apparently said it was up to the group to decide. This manœuvre seemed a little too complicated for Peter, so I backed out.

Hygiene again on Sunday. We were all ordered out to scrub the walls in the corridor and kitchen. This job lasted five hours.

Wednesday, April 13

Sasha dropped in on Monday. He talked a little about his studies at the Institute for Foreign Languages (a kind of institute on its own here in Moscow). At present he was interested in Norwegian foreign politics as he had to take an examination on the subject in the autumn. He nevertheless complained bitterly because the only source he had was a book by Jacob Friis. We gave him Tim Greve's booklet in English, and a copy of the *New York Times* which had a lengthy article on the free trade area.

He said that the Institute was near the American Embassy, but he wouldn't say how many students were there. The Russians seem to have a mania for keeping everything secret. Most of the students at this Institute enter the Foreign Ministry.

As a matter of fact, we had some difficulty in getting him into the University. There is a rule which stipulates that visitors from Moscow are allowed in only on Saturdays and Sundays. However, after visiting various offices, Ingjald got him permission. It is surprising what one can achieve if one is prepared to make a row.

At Tuesday's lecture Peter told me that the group

meeting on Lenin lasted two hours. First, a student had addressed them on the "Education of Lenin", and on how necessary it was to keep students busy at all times, teaching them a true understanding of work and life, and of collectivisation, etc. Peter got up and expressed his irritation at the inadequate contact between life and study which had been exemplified by the speech. That particular student, like all the rest, had been guilty of extensive shirking of compulsory lectures. I asked him what they said about his criticisms. He said they had nothing sensible to say.

He tried rather weakly to defend the personality cult of Lenin, saying that human beings must have someone to worship, and in the long run it really did not matter whether they worshipped Christ or Lenin.

In the evening we visited a Western girl, who was entertaining two lively Georgian girl students, and a Nigerian student who was in his second year of medicine. Before coming to Moscow he had studied in Canada, but had felt Communism had much to offer. Consequently—and in spite of warnings—he had come to Russia.

During the two years he had been here, however, he had had many severe shocks. The lack of honesty which characterises Soviet society—the fact that on one hand they engage in all sorts of dirty commercial transactions and on the other try to appear great, powerful, and completely righteous, had made a very bad impression on him.

He also talked of the general atmosphere of suspicion (this we shared), and of the unnatural way in which the Russians lived together in the collective without freedom and without the right to private ownership.

The proposed Friendship University had also

failed to exert any attraction for him. One could not but doubt the Soviet's honourable intentions, he said, when one could see how much lying and emptiness there was in this society.

Moreover, he added, one could not help feeling sceptical about all their talk of peace and friendship when one realised that behind it was a system bent on expanding.

To crown all this, he went on to mention cases of racial discrimination. For example, he knew of one Russian girl student whose name had been taken for having in all innocence visited his room. He got quite worked up about the Russians, and as we wandered back over the campus after the party, with the vast shadow of the University colossus over our shoulders, my last impression is of him muttering intensely several times:

"They can't win! They can't win!"

Friday, April 15

On Tuesday evening Peter and I went to a student revue at the House of Culture. Peter talked a little about himself. He told me that he had been a commercial traveller for two years and had a salary of around 1,500 roubles a month. Usually, older and more experienced people got jobs like this, though they were pretty scarce as the director or an engineer often did the travelling.

After this he began to study at the University of Perm, but had been sent down through trouble with women—that was the allegation, anyway. He had also been expelled from the Komsomol, the Soviet Youth Organisation. However, with the help of contacts, he had managed to get accepted for Moscow University. For one summer he worked hard as an agitator and was re-admitted as a Komsomol member.

When I went for my tutorial on Thursday I was kept waiting rather a long time. At last the teacher came running in to say that he had been delayed at a disputation for a doctorate. Unfortunately there could be no tutorial today.

In the evening I went to the club house in the Lenin Hills, with Alexander, and watched a cabaret produced by the physics students. It began by a student declaiming at immense length about something Gorky had written on Lenin. The audience was clearly bored. In the interval a girl from the Committee of Management asked us what we thought of it, to which Alexander replied that the first item had gone on a bit too long. The girl answered very apologetically and said they felt they had to have something about Lenin.

Then followed songs and sketches. One of the sketches consisted of three tableaux: the first illustrating a mathematics lecture—many empty seats, two students asleep; the second a physics lecture— more sleeping students; the third a lecture on the history of the Communist Party—a large number of students asleep (and great applause from the audience!).

Wednesday, April 20

On Friday I had a visit from Evgenii Maximov, who lives on this floor. He was one of the people who had done most of the talking during our recent big discussion on the meaning of freedom. Now he wanted to know a little more about Scandinavia. I gave him several brochures.

On Saturday evening Ingjald and I were invited to visit the Georgian girls. They had laid on a big junket with lots of Georgian wines and delicacies. The party got pretty lively and there were songs and anecdotes. One of the stories we heard is worth repeating as a typical comment on Soviet society. It went like this. . .

Three friends sat together in a railway compartment. After a long spell of silence, one of them said "Yes". Pause. The next one said "Yes". Pause. And then the third one said: "Oh, why don't we stop talking politics?"

We were pretty late returning to our room. On the way we met one of the Polish students, Sbychek, from our corridor. He came in, sat down and talked for ages. He said he had almost finished his final thesis at the Faculty of Physics. He had been given a very big grant for his studies and had had eight people to help him. He hoped to be able to go to England to continue his education.

Then he started to talk about new Russian long-distance rockets. These, he said, were powered by a new Russian fuel which was extremely dangerous. The rockets, he alleged, were continuously aimed at different targets. The new fuel began to crystallise after one month—and then became self-igniting unless it was removed in the meantime.

If he can be believed we are certainly living on borrowed time!

A Russian living on this floor told me the Pole had been born a count. He was not popular among his fellow-students because they said he was unreliable, but professionally he was considered to be very competent.

On Tuesday Peter and I arranged to go to the Lenin meeting to commemorate the approaching 90th anniversary of his birth. Peter turned up with a Tartar girl named Limosa. During the very tedious meeting that followed at the University, Limosa asked me whether I thought there would be a Communist régime in Norway. She was astounded when I replied that I neither believed it nor hoped for it. I added that this was not such a strange idea since I was a Conservative. She stared at me with eyes as round as saucers and said it was the first time she had ever seen such a creature!

Saturday, April 23

Today I had another talk with Peter, who told me he had been trying to get a summer job as a Pioneer Leader at a Black Sea resort. Unfortunately he had applied too late. He could get a similar job in Moscow but wasn't interested. The Pioneers are the Communist children's organisation. It enables the Communists to get at children while they're still at school. Later they can graduate to the Komsomol. A job as a Pioneer Leader, I gathered, gives a salary of about 400 roubles a month, plus free board and lodging—which was reckoned to be pretty good for the summer. Another of his plans was to go with a group of students to the Archangel area to study dialects. I said what about my joining the party? Peter didn't think it could be fixed up, but promised to ask the leader of the group.

Tuesday, April 26

On Sunday we took a stroll around the neighbouring Moscow suburbs. The outlook was pretty grim. Masses of people, terrible filth, and houses like barracks. This is a side of Moscow people don't hear about—and little wonder! In the evening I went with Peter to the theatre in the Sovietskaya Hotel. This is a new little theatre, and consists entirely of young actors. We saw a modern Soviet play called "Five Evenings". The production was quite unconventional. The decorations were stylised, and much use was made of light effects, while virtually dispensing with props. So far as I could gather, the drift of the play was that love is something which concerns the two persons involved, and not the rest of society—not a very Communist doctrine.

After a very elementary lecture today Peter declared that Pustavoyt was useless and that he had no influence in the Faculty. The really powerful figure was the Dean—Samarin. Peter said that if one wanted to be a professor in the Soviet Union one had to actively support the régime. I said this was a strange system and that we had nothing like it in Norway, to which Peter replied that it nevertheless had its points. And he added with an ironic chuckle: "We all agree with each other".

By and large I must admit that Peter has an astonishingly objective and rather charming attitude to the Soviet system. I think he may well be typical of many Soviet students. Albert, for example, is more or less of the same type—a person with considerable intelligence and great adaptability.

And no wish to be a martyr. . .

They perhaps smile a little at the propaganda and

the various cults; they shrug their shoulders at the eternal schooling of the authorities. But they also play the rôle of agitator when it is necessary for them to retain their reputation as good Soviet citizens.

Their attitude towards the régime is not one of opposition. It is more of a passive nature. Regarding the Western world they have limited opinions, though some of those they do have are in the main correct and objective. Yet by and large, this is a world far away from them.

And if one day they are urged in the name of Lenin to go out to defend the Soviet Union, Communism and the future of mankind against Western imperialists, they will do so.

I suppose most of us would do exactly the same thing if we were in their shoes. The old story . . . one's attitude is relative to one's environment, good or bad, right or wrong.

On Wednesday Sbychek, the Polish student, went with me to Moscow. He had heard that there were some early paintings by Segall and Kandinski in the Tretyakov Gallery. Naturally not everybody is permitted to view this collection. The general public cannot go in at all, for it seems that Segall and Kandinski absolutely reek of "bourgeois" influences. Sbychek must have been showing his inherent nobility by wanting to see it, and he was convinced that we could wangle our way in. We couldn't. We were told that only those who were studying "aesthetics" and who could get a chit from the University saying that it was necessary for their studies, would be allowed in.

On Thursday Pustavoyt asked if I had any plans for May Day. When I replied that I had, his sigh of relief was almost audible. Nobody, he told me, could be alone on May 1—they must all be in the collective.

The same evening Peter and I went to see the Bakchisarai Fountain Ballet at the Bolshoi Theatre.

BATTLE WITH BUREAUCRACY

Sunday, May 1

May Day! We had to get up at seven o'clock this morning to catch a bus allocated to foreign students who had received tickets for the stand on Red Square during the celebrations. Ingjald and I had started out too late to get tickets but thought we would be able to get on without them. Nikoforov was in the bus and gave us tickets made out to a couple of Finnish students who hadn't turned up.

The bus drove past the first of the three police barriers but at the second we were asked to produce our passports and tickets. Naturally in our case the two documents didn't match up and we were not allowed through. Nikoforov tried to explain the situation, though without very much enthusiasm or concern.

We tried to get through at another point, but failed again. So we stood in the crowd and had a very good view of the military parade and demonstrations. These lasted three hours and consisted almost entirely of Red Flags and masses of banners of Lenin.

During the demonstrations we got into conversation with some Russians. One of them, a workman, was a bit drunk and very indignant that he, a Soviet citizen—a toiler—wasn't allowed into Red Square. In fact, he was well and truly fed up with

Symbol of a worker outside Tretyakov Gallery, Moscow. Inside, students view a painting by Ivanov.

everything and everybody, especially the bosses who decided it all.

Another Russian was tremendously thirsty for any factual information about the West. What surprised him particularly was that enlightened people still believed in God. Finally there was a nasty, arrogant type who was only interested in his own opinions.

Tuesday, May 3

Yesterday at the Lenin Library Metro Station they unveiled a beautiful mosaic of . . . Lenin, naturally. In Russia man does not live by bread alone!

At Saturday's lecture our teacher spoke about the poet Chuchev. I found it remarkably objective.

He began by mentioning that some critics in the Stalin era had characterised Chuchev as "not far from being a revolutionary". In fact Chuchev was a true conservative as well as a great poet (Tolstoy called him the greatest Russian poet). Obviously Chuchev was too important a figure to be dismissed as a reactionary, which meant that a few years ago the critics had to characterise him as a near revolutionary. Today Russian critics can make concessions to Chuchev's political views and at the same time honour his literary works. Can this be a little proof that time is working in the desired direction to produce a more liberal attitude towards men of Chuchev's calibre? I hope so.

Also on Saturday Peter told me that his mother's bungalow just outside Moscow had burned down. They had had a good collection of books . . . all lost. Everything was insured, but unfortunately not for its full value. The bungalow had been about 80 square metres in size and worth at least 100,000 roubles, Peter said. As a result of this he had been released from his lectures. Moreover, he can occupy a single room in the so-called Recreation Department on Lenin Hills.

That evening Ingjald and I looked up our Georgian girl friends again. There was another big party with lots of good food, including Caucasian trout (delicious), and good wines, too. We danced until long past midnight, and I got on famously with a sweet little number called Ariadne.

Peter came in again today and we talked about linguistics.

Friday, May 6

I saw Ariadne again. Her charming head contains absolutely no anti-Communist ideas and so I'm doing my best to plant a few there. She mentioned that there was talk of knocking two single apartments into one and putting two students into them. Apparently, experience has shown, students work better when several of them share the same room. But the possibility of mutual surveillance didn't much appeal to me and I had a few choice remarks to make about this idea.

On Thursday Sasha Sorokin, his wife, Ingjald and I went to the theatre to see "A Story from Irkutsk". The basic plot dealt with a labour brigade working on a power station in Siberia. The moral of the piece was, briefly, that co-operation and the personal contribution of labour created well-being and happiness—which isn't a bad moral after all. We were also shown how a really successful Communist family should live and we were assured that "all people on earth should live happily, particularly those who are building Communism". The production and acting were first class.

On the way home Sasha amplified the message of the play by adding that Lenin had said that when Communism was fully achieved all the lavatories would be built of gold.

To judge by the lavatories of present-day Russia they're still a long way from completing Communism!

Today Ingjald and I saw Nikoforov to discuss travel plans. Ingjald had already tried hard to get permission to visit the new agricultural territories but had not been successful.

We told Nikoforov that we wanted to visit the Caucasus and I added that I would like to return to Norway via Murmansk. Nikoforov was very friendly and said that this was possible.

However, on reflection, he said the trip via Murmansk *might* be a bit troublesome as he understood there was no regular passenger route between Murmansk and Northern Norway. We pointed out that a railway line ran almost to the frontier, but Nikoforov said that it would be very difficult to cross the frontier by road as people were not easily allowed into frontier areas.

Finally, he said it was not absolutely certain one could get even to Murmansk, as there might be some military manœuvres going on in that area at the time.

Having been so helpful, he wrote down our preferences and promised to see what could be done. As far as choosing a Southern route was concerned, we had better get in touch with Intourist, he advised.

Monday, May 9

On Saturday we trooped into the Intourist Head Office in Gorki Street, and were told to go to the bureau at the Hotel National. We went to the Hotel National, and there they referred us back to the Head Office. At last we got hold of a woman who listened to our requests. She explained that Inrourist only arranged "tourist trips" costing a minimum of 12 dollars a day excluding transport. And there was no means of paying this in roubles. We said that this was far beyond our resources, to which she retorted that in that case Intourist could do nothing for us and we'd better see Nikoforov again.

We asked her the cost of air and rail tickets and hotel accommodation. She said she had no information about these matters—at Intourist Head Office! —and advised us to ask at the tourist bureau in the Hotel Metropol. Ingjald went there while I went to my lecture.

At the lecture I found there couldn't have been more than 20 per cent of those obliged to attend. It was a talk on Russian literature in the 19th Century and pretty dull anyway. But the lecturer, who wasn't blind either, said that the students would either attend his lectures or he would stop giving them. If that happened, he warned, he would have to notify the Party Bureau.

I remember a Russian student telling me recently of a group of students who had complained to the University authorities that a certain lecturer was treating them like children. He had, for example, made a row when students arrived late or did not appear to be following the lecture. The result was that the lecturer disappeared.

On Saturday evening I visited the Americans. They are very concerned about an American aircraft that has just been shot down over the Soviet Union. But the situation is confused at the moment. The Russian students are also quite interested in the affair but I haven't noticed any particular annoyance on their part.

Albert called in to see me . . . to gloat. With malicious glee he had pounced on the news. Ha-ha, he said, now we can all see for ourselves what an aggressive crowd NATO is, and yet it is supposed to be only a defensive organisation. What about that?

Nobody seems to have any apprehension about war breaking out. In general one comes across much less fear of war here than in the West. This, of course, is due to the fact that the propaganda machine does not burden itself with any prognostications of defeat.

That evening Ingjald went to see a comic opera which the students at the Faculty of Science had produced in connection with the "annual celebration of the birth of Archimedes". The theme was the small problems of student life translated into the world of the Greek Gods.

Friday, May 13

At the language lesson on Wednesday we were given the task of writing a piece on the theme "15 years after the war". I used the opportunity to write my views on the Cold War, the universal Pharisaic attitude and the general phony moral pathos of the times. I thought the last point was particularly valid in view of the American aircraft incident.

After I'd written it and handed it in I became rather apprehensive about the way it would be received. To my surprise Madame Rassodova didn't react at all. She merely pointed out the technical faults and let it pass.

Later Peter and I went to see the big new Russian film "New Earth". There was plenty of good stuff in it, but terribly long drawn out. After the show we had a steak at a restaurant. It was so late we couldn't get into one restaurant we tried, even though we attempted to bribe the doorman.

Yesterday Ingjald and I went down to see the Youth Committee—our official hosts—to sound them out about our travel plans. We met Sorokin, charming as ever though a bit shifty. First we asked if there was any chance of our getting a travel grant. There wasn't much. British and American students each get 1,500 roubles, but this is probably due to the fact that Soviet students have relatively better conditions in England and America. In the United States, for example, they get 200 dollars a month.

Sorokin mumbled something to the effect that even though the exchange scheme hadn't included any travel grants, he might be able to wangle a grant from the funds of the Student Council.

This seems a little peculiar, but possibly he wants to arrange matters in some way that suits the Russians' book—perhaps a step towards getting these student exchanges under the thumb of the Communist-controlled International Union of Students. It is true, however, that we have no right to ask for a travel grant.

We put our travel plans in front of him—Caucasus, Crimea, Kiev, possibly Riga and Leningrad. We also inquired—in spite of Nikoforov's cautions —about the possibilities of going home via Murmansk. Sorokin said immediately there was no chance of being allowed to cross the frontier. Passenger communications, he pointed out, must run via the official crossing points and no exception could be made. I then said that in any case we would like to visit Murmansk as it would be useful to me in my studies. Sorokin agreed to do what he could to help.

Sunday, May 15

After the lecture on Saturday Peter introduced me to a girl student of the same year, Maria, and we all went to a restaurant in Gorki-street. There we ate ice-cream and drank champagne. Maria said she thought that people in capitalist Norway must all be egotists. Only in the USSR were people brought up to think of one another. Furthermore, in this country the State gave people something to live for. She simply could not understand what people lived for in a capitalist community.

She believed the capitalist countries gave people nothing to fight for, so they merely fought for themselves. Preoccupations with family life, too, tended to isolate people from one another. She evidently didn't think much of family life.

I was smart enough to put an end to this line by using a well-tried and successful gambit. I suggested with an innocent face that she should go to the West and see for herself how egotistically people lived.

As usual, her reaction was regret that travel was not possible.

Sunday, May 22

I had lunch at a restaurant in town, and saw an older student whom I had met before. He had been a soldier for many years before he came to the University. He had been stationed at many places all over the Soviet Union, and he knew how much poverty and misery and emptiness there was in this society. Once, he had believed in the system. He had believed in it for a long time.

It was not until he had come to the University that he had begun to realise the hollowness of the propaganda. Now he believed that freedom of thought and speech were the most important freedoms of all; that it was almost a condition for any other form of freedom.

He told me he had bought himself a powerful radio set and listened regularly to the *Voice of America*. A couple of times his aerial had been cut down—by whom he didn't know. Otherwise he hadn't any trouble. He didn't have much to do with the other students and very rarely discussed politics.

He had a wife and children who lived outside Moscow, and he earned a pretty decent living as a photographer during the vacations and free time. He went off on his bicycle and toured the towns around Moscow. He would call at schools and offer to take photographs of the classes. The whole thing was a rare private enterprise. By next year, he said, he would have saved enough money to buy a car, and he could then cast his net wider.

Nonetheless, he admitted to being one of the relatively few people who constantly suffered under the pressure of a totalitarian régime, and he pictured the West as a paradise.

He talked of the frequent arguments about full and free employment in the USSR. Unemployment, he said, was prevented by completely artificial means. The authorities merely employed far too many people on a particular job and paid them minimum wages. As an example, he mentioned the three charwomen employed in our corridor at the University. They were on the payroll in spite of the fact that it was the students' job to clean out their own rooms.

I said little during his outburst. Perhaps it did him good to get it all off his chest, but on the other hand it was just possible he was trying to be provocative. I don't believe the latter is likely, but one must always bear the possibility in mind.

I showed him some American magazines, and they made quite an impression on him. He whispered several times, almost in ecstasy: "Yes, this is freedom. Of course this is freedom".

Finally I thought it my duty to tell him that even though I believed everything was better in the West, it was still a long way from being a paradise. Maybe I should have held my tongue and let him keep his illusions. He had exchanged his faith in the Communist millennium for a faith in a Western paradise.

Was there any chance of him finding a third alternative which would help him to escape from the colourless daily Soviet life ?

Ah, well . . . I didn't destroy *all* his illusions!

On the way out I asked him if he were not afraid

A corner of Sejersted's room. Below: Ornamental gates in one part of the University.

the room was "miked". I mentioned that I'd heard microphones had been found in the walls of embassies. This didn't seem to worry him, and I was rather annoyed with myself for having interrupted his conversation.

On Monday I went to see *Death of a Salesman* by the American dramatist Arthur Miller. A good deal of Western literature is translated into Russian. But it is very carefully selected. *Death of a Salesman* is a typical example, since it contains Miller's pungent criticism of certain aspects of Western society. The play was performed by student amateurs in the club house on Lenin Hills. It was very well done, too.

May 17—Tuesday—was a very busy day. In the morning we called on Sorokin, who told us that he had made inquiries about the various places we wished to visit—but that unfortunately all the hotels were booked up. He would, however, try another couple of places, but the chances were pretty slim. Of the two alternatives for the Murmansk trip he had heard nothing. He said he would like us to keep in touch with him.

I suspect friend Sorokin is using delaying tactics and that finally it will be too late to do anything at all if he keeps it going long enough.

On Thursday May 19 we telephoned him again to see how things stood. He said he would be only too happy to see us. But unfortunately he had not been able to arrange anything, so we would have to see Nikoforov once again.

On Saturday we visited the Finnish exhibition and had our photographs taken by a Finn who was doing an illustrated piece about Scandinavians at the show. Then I went to an exhibition of paintings by an Indian artist of Russian origin named Rerik. This exhibition has attracted a lot of attention—and rightly so. The paintings are very colourful and some of them highly original in conception. It is said that Khrushchev likes them too. Afterwards I gave my friend Maria some hints on the Swedish language, which she is evidently keen on learning.

Today I tried to borrow a bicycle, but I began this operation too late. Only racing cycles were available, and to obtain one I had to have a chit signed by one of my tutors. I pottered about instead.

Saturday, May 28

On Tuesday (May 24) Ingjald and I went to see Nikoforov about our trip. He wrote down the proposed routes but thought we wouldn't make it as the hotels were bound to be full. He added that about four million tourists travelled to the south during the summer. Nevertheless he would try.

I again brought up the idea of going home via Murmansk and Kirkenes. Nikoforov said he had found out that this would be right out of the question, but a trip to and from Murmansk might be possible.

He then steered the conversation round to the American spy plane and Norway's rôle in this. And for nearly two hours he kept us in his office while he explained—sometimes vehemently and with lots of gesticulation—how aggressive and frightful the Americans were, how this was clearly aggression and espionage, and how right Comrade Khrushchev had been to make such a fuss at the Summit Conference in Paris.

He loved Grieg, Nikoforov went on, and he loved Norwegian nature. He had always believed that the

Norwegians were a strong and independent people. It had therefore come as a tremendous shock to him when Norway had completely sold herself to the American imperialists by joining NATO—that aggressive organisation—and permitting American troops to enter the country.

This was absolutely unnecessary, he declared. Sweden for example, had not done so (there was no chance to argue the question of Sweden's neutrality).

Nikoforov then explained how, shortly after the war, the United States had started the Cold War, how their one desire was to exterminate the Soviet Union, and how they had continued ever since to arm and build bases with which to encircle the USSR.

But it must be borne in mind, he warned, that the Soviet Union was stronger. Her rockets had now made the US bases worthless.

Then he became fatherly. He told us he was already a grown man when the Cold War started, so that he was in a position to put us right about its background.

He realised, he said, that we were under considerable pressure from Western propaganda, but he nevertheless hoped that one day we would see things in their proper light.

We were unsure of our ground. Neither of us was very keen to start an argument with him so we let him babble on. But finally he irritated Ingjald so much that things ended up on a lively note.

During Nikoforov's dissertation the phone rang several times. He answered the calls merely to say he was so busy he had no time to talk.

We have since heard that an American student had a similar experience lasting 45 minutes. So far as the Americans knew, Nikoforov had never before gone in for this sort of political lecturing. We left

Nikoforov in a somewhat pessimistic frame of mind as far as our travel plans were concerned.

It looks as though the Soviet attitude to the spy plane business is getting in the way of our own arrangements.

On Thursday we took a trip to Yasnaya Polyana, the estate of Tolstoy. The excursion had been arranged by the Language Institute and we were certainly an international crowd. We were transported in an unusually ancient and broken-down bus which took five hours to get us there. The trip was highly successful—it was the first real summer day we have had and the vast natural park was most impressive. We saw the grave of Tolstoy—one of the giants of Russian literature—a simple mound of earth beneath tall trees.

In the evening Peter called again.

Today we went back to see Nikoforov to discuss the travel situation. With very little hope and after waiting an hour in his ante-room we were ushered in to the presence.

Nikoforov came straight to the point. "I've decided to help you in your trip south", he said, and from the tone of his voice there was little doubt that everything had been fixed.

The whole procedure is so typical! It's clear as daylight that all the talk about the hotels being full was just a blind while a political decision about our trip was being taken. We had realised this the whole time—and what is more Nikoforov knew that we knew. However, it had now been decided that we were to be given help—as if it were not completely natural that a foreign department should help a foreign student!

He prefaced his announcement with the statement that we were being helped on our way because he believed that, after all, we were not as bad as the Americans. He hoped that we would take back with us an objective view of Soviet realities, that we would learn to judge a nation by its honest endeavours, and that this feeling would ripen in us as scientists of the future.

We should always try, he said, to find the inner meaning of the Russian people, and was glad that we were trying to do it.

Comparison with the Americans is a typical Soviet reflex action. American travel possibilities have been drastically curtailed since the aircraft incident. It is true that they are being allowed to make a group excursion to the south, but that is all. Some of them wanted a three-day trip to Leningrad to look at the town, but that has been cancelled. A fishery expert who had been promised a trip to Murmansk has now been refused.

But we are evidently all right. We have been graciously informed that we are not as bad as the Americans, so our arrangements are on!

THE LONG WAY HOME

Wednesday, June 1

Once again I have been to see Nikoforov. This time I called to ask about a permit for a trip to Vladimir I wish to make at Whitsuntide. After waiting some time, and after a discussion with a few of his office staff as to whether I could or could not be allowed in to see the boss, I finally made it and produced my plan for the Vladimir trip. Nikoforov said shortly that the trip was not possible at present. I said that was odd and what was the reason? He came up with the old chestnut about some Germans having booked all the hotel accommodation.

I asked him about Murmansk and reminded him that he himself had said that although it was impossible to cross the frontier in the north it might well be possible to do the trip to Leningrad-Murmansk and back. Having thought about this plan, I told him, I was all in favour of it, especially as it would help me in my studies.

The reply was a blank refusal without any explanation.

I have begun to feel we are back on our old status of being "as bad as the Americans".

To have enough time for our trip to the south I asked if we could have our residence permits extended for a couple of days. Nikoforov replied: "Surely you can leave Moscow for the south a few days earlier?" Finally I asked how and when we could get our exit permits. This problem also seemed full of complications.

It appeared the difficulty was that we would not be going home via Moscow! His office usually organised exit visas for foreign students, but we would have to get ours in Leningrad.

In fact he will not hand us our exit permits without getting in exchange our residence permits, and consequently we cannot get our exit permits until we leave for the south.

On Sunday evening I called on Peter in his new flat and drank some Rumanian wine with him. He gave me a present of several books.

It has been announced, incidentally, that as from next year boys and girls will be segregated and housed on their own floors. The present mixing is to end. The reason is quite clear—immorality and noise.

However, the students have reacted spontaneously against this decree and there was a mass meeting on this floor the other day as a kind of protest. According to a conversation I overheard in the lift this seems to have become a minor revolution.

Friday, June 3

Ingjald is busy on a small paper he wants to hand in to his faculty as a kind of final contribution. I don't feel inclined to submit anything, though I have been handing in analyses and comments to my professor.

On Thursday I went for my usual consultation, but Pustavoyt wasn't around. Instead I met Maria who had just been taking an examination in dialectical materialism. "A terrible sweat", she said—but she had passed with flying colours. I congratulated her, to which she replied that such successes were by no means due to any merit but depended on one's relations with the professor.

Practically all examinations here are purely oral. I told her about the Western system of written examinations in which personal relationships with professors were of no importance. She said our system must be perfect in every way—but there was irony in her voice. Then she attacked me for having "come to the Soviet Union with a prejudiced point of view". She had recently met an American who didn't have these prejudices, she said. He had been thrilled by what he had seen and had praised the Metro and the new building effort.

I apologised for having failed to show appreciation for these things in front of her, and asked whether criticism meant only that one was prejudiced. No, she wouldn't agree to that either. It wasn't nice of me to talk like this to such a sweet girl!

Friday, June 10

It is now awfully warm. We have been chasing around the town preparing everything for our trip. Nothing, however, has been achieved—and Nikoforov has disappeared without trace. And to think we were planning to leave in a few days' time!

Last Friday I went with Maria to see *Carmen* at the Bolshoi. The performance was very good apart from the toreador, who was short and sang badly.

Afterwards we talked politics for a time. I confused her by asking how it was possible to have a democracy and a dictatorship of the proletariat at the same time? She said that democracy was for the majority, while the dictatorship was only for a minority. Furthermore, full freedom of speech existed in the USSR, she said—except for those who were against the regime! Perhaps my comments on this argument were a little too sarcastic; but I have the impression she became a little thoughtful about the validity of her own argument. What is noteworthy is that she could have given a better answer—the "correct" one would surely have been that, since the Soviet Union had become a classless society, no minority classes could any longer exist in it. And as no one is against the Government, there cannot of course be any question of dictatorship!

Back in my room I heard that the Foreign Bureau had been trying to get me on the 'phone. They rang again on Saturday morning and asked me to drop in.

I was shown straight in to Nikoforov, who received me with a pleasant smile and asked if it was I who had been inquiring about a trip to Vladimir. When I confirmed it was he said that it would be arranged. It seems as though Norwegians aren't as bad as Americans after all! Nonetheless he became a little thoughtful when I pointed out that I had originally intended to leave for Vladimir the same afternoon.

He wrote out a quick note to the manager of an hotel in Vladimir, who happened to be an old acquaintance of his, and a letter to the Registration Bureau in central Moscow where I would have to go to get the necessary stamp put on my residence permit. It took me a long time to find this office. Later I rang Peter and suggested that he might like to come along to Vladimir with me.

We met after lunch and went down to the railway station. There we were told that all the tickets for the first train had been sold, and that we would have to wait about four hours for the next. Fortunately Peter had a brainwave. He suggested we should take a suburban train to Petushki, which was about half way there, and take the first train from Petushki to Vladimir. The plan worked perfectly and we had an hour's pleasant stroll through the streets of Petushki.

It seemed to be a typical Russian town with cows in the streets, kolkhozes in the centre and numerous small, tumbledown buildings around them. The most interesting place I saw was the town grocer's, which sold Norwegian herring. Otherwise the shops were among the most awful things one can encounter.

They were like the shops everywhere in the country-side—unattractive and having a very poor range of goods.

We arrived in Vladimir fairly late in the afternoon. We ate in the railway restaurant and went from there to the hotel, which is one of the largest and smartest looking buildings in the town. The town is situated on a charming and picturesque brow of a hill. It is very old and has been the seat of once-powerful princes. Now it is a military centre, but still renowned for its cathedral. Peter and I walked around the town before going to bed.

Next day we went to the cathedral to watch the Whitsuntide celebrations. The cathedral was packed, and many people who had been unable to get inside crowded on the steps by the doors. Most of them were old women, and they gladly made way for Peter and I so that we managed to squeeze ourselves inside.

The cathedral was decorated with masses of green foliage in keeping with the Whitsun custom. Many people carried candles which they wanted to place in the candlesticks, but the crowd was so thick it was impossible to move. So they passed the candles from hand to hand.

Alms were also sent out to the crowd of beggars who had gathered outside the cathedral doors. This was the only place in the Soviet Union where I saw such a relatively large number of beggars.

Afterwards we had another look at the town and went back to the hotel for lunch. At the same time we inquired about the trains back to Moscow and were told that the only one left at 1 a.m. We then asked about buses and the so-called taxi-buses. There were plenty of these but we were told that foreigners were only allowed to travel by train.

After this astonishing piece of news we went down to the bus station to see if it was a fact. We spent about two hours there trying to get a lift to Moscow, but it looked as though the hotel staff had told us the truth.

We were given all sorts of excuses by bus and taxi-drivers. As far as we could make out, there were two men who tipped off the drivers about us as soon as they arrived at the station. Finally, when we could find no means of transport, we became really fed up.

The worst thing was that Peter had begun to get worried. He confided that he really ought to have told the University Party Bureau that he was going to take a trip with a foreigner, and he hadn't done so. He was hoping he wouldn't get into trouble. I asked him if he'd had any trouble through spending so much time with me. He said that on one occasion one of the chief agitators had asked him what we talked so much about. He had replied that he was telling me how to get around at the University, and since then there had been no more questions.

Eventually we took a train into Petushki to see if we could go on from there to Moscow. We arrived at midnight—and naturally the last suburban train had gone ages before.

We were therefore compelled to spend three hours in a filthy little waiting room which was packed. But it turned out to be an enjoyable spell of waiting since the people in the waiting room turned out to be a most entertaining band of gypsies, several peasants and a mushroom gatherer—in general the most motley crowd one could imagine. Everybody tried to sleep but at regular intervals they were awakened by a policeman who said it was forbidden to sleep in the waiting room. At 3 a.m.

we finally crushed our way into an overloaded train and got to Moscow, where we grabbed the first taxi and went straight to the Lenin Hills.

It was 6 a.m. when I arrived at the University, and my troubles weren't over yet. None of the lifts were working and the staircase had been locked.

I seemed to be running around for ages before I was able to arouse a sleeping "watchman" who told me how I could arrange to get a lift working. When the lift started I hopped in, but it shuddered to a stop between the 13th and 14th floors and I was stuck there for a quarter of an hour.

On Tuesday we called again at the Foreign Bureau and were given a note to the Registration Bureau, stating that we wanted to travel to the various places mentioned and that we would like to have our exit permits at the same time.

From Nikoforov's office we went straight to the Danish Embassy, to which we had been invited to celebrate the Danish National Day. We arrived rather early and were shown into one of the inner rooms so that other people could follow us. One of the first to enter was Nikolai Ignatov of the Soviet Presidium, a VIP who was flanked by secretaries and interpreters. He gave a friendly greeting to everyone in the room, including ourselves. We told him we were Norwegian students and he smiled broadly. Our conversation with him lasted about 20 minutes. He seemed a friendly and avuncular type, and we chatted mainly about our studies in the University and our plans for a trip to the south.

Ignatov mentioned that I could easily pass for a Russian as far as my appearance was concerned— and this certainly was a compliment. Finally he introduced us to Marshal Budenny, who wore an enormous moustache and a breastful of medals. We had a few words with him, also.

Later we heard we'd been a sensation at the party. Numerous ambassadors and diplomats had been craning their necks in the background while we had been having our talk with Ignatov. They had been trying to find out who these young men were and why Ignatov had been talking to them for so long.

On Wednesday there was an exam. We met at the Institute at noon and first wrote an essay on "Why I like Chekhov". Ingjald re-wrote his piece: "Meeting With the People of Moscow". After that we were asked questions on Russian grammar—pretty difficult ones. The whole thing took about three and a half hours. This was a special examination for Ingjald and me, and Madame Rassodovo, who went through our work as soon as it was completed, seemed very pleased. She told me later that she had talked to Alexeev about the ban on foreigners travelling from Vladimir by any other means than by rail. Alexeev was astonished by this. Finally, she gave us each a present and said she would miss us. This was really nice of her. We have not been particularly diligent students, but we have always enjoyed our lessons with her and it has been a pleasure to work with her.

On Thursday I managed to get to the Registration Bureau with the note from Nikoforov. It had to be the one day the office was closed. Afterwards I went to see Pustavoyt, whom I haven't seen for three weeks. But he was still missing.

Today—Friday—has been extremely busy. First we called in on Nikoforov to get a chit for Intourist so that we can order hotel accommodation for our trip. We were not really entitled to get this paper

The main tower of Moscow University.

Author Francis Sejersted, fur hatted, stands at the entrance to the Faculty of Philology.

from Nikoforov until we had received our travel permit from the Registration Bureau, but since this permit has been delayed for some reason or other, we must get cracking with our hotel reservations. Naturally we failed to get any paper from Nikoforov —first, because he wasn't in his office, and, secondly, because the registration office wanted a detailed itinerary of our route with exact times of arrival and departure.

We dashed off to Moscow, first to the Registration Bureau, where it took one and a half hours to get some attention. They started off by saying they couldn't give us our exit permits straight away, but promised eventually to issue these with our travel permits on Monday.

From the Registration Bureau we went to Intourist, where we had to produce a detailed plan of our route. Then we had to go to two different offices to find out about air and rail connections. At both places the service was slow and unpleasant.

However, armed with this information we returned to Nikoforov's office to get that desperately needed paper so that we could make our hotel reservations. We had been told he would be in his office at 4 p.m. Of course he was not. His lady clerk simply said that it would be impossible to make hotel reservations for the times in question, but since Nikoforov himself had promised us it could be done we wanted to see him personally.

In town we tried to get the last instalment of our grant, but were put off again. For this one required certificates from the Students' Home and the Faculty. We looked in on Alexeev and asked if he could help us but he was very busy and couldn't see us until tomorrow, Saturday.

Saturday, June 11

Saturday morning—and the situation is critical. Nothing is in order, we've made hardly any progress through all the formalities, and we were planning to leave on Tuesday! Nikoforov continues to be invisible. At his office they say they haven't a clue where he is, and of course it's impossible to make any hotel booking without a letter from him. The question is whether we can go without having booked hotels, assuming we can get our travel permits and tickets. But we've neither of these yet.

Pustavoyt is also still in the middle of his vanishing trick. I am beginning to wonder if there hasn't been a little purge. . .?

Sunday, June 12

I have just finished packing and have decided to send my books and gramophone records home and my bags to Leningrad. The only problem is where to find an address in Leningrad to which we can send them, not knowing where we stand about hotels. Despite the fact that we are still without our travel permits, exit permits, air tickets and hotel rooms, we are still being optimistic enough to think we have a chance of getting away on Tuesday.

Yesterday was also a busy day. Nikoforov made another appearance and announced that of course our journey would be on—hadn't he himself promised it? Then he came back to a familiar theme. The Norwegian Government, he said, had behaved very correctly over the American aircraft intermezzo, so naturally we could go.

We gave him our detailed itinerary and he

promised to have the notifications ready for Monday. We went on to the Embassy to pick up some money that had been sent from home.

Next we called on Alexeev, who referred us to the Faculty in order to get a certificate to the effect that we were leaving the University. We dashed to the Institute to say goodbye to Madame Rassodova, and gave her a book about Norway and some chocolates. She seemed pleased.

We hurried on to the Faculty, where I finally ran Pustavoyt to earth and took a fond farewell. From my old friend Tokmakov I received what was called the "Obkhodnoy List" that Alexeev had talked about. On this I was supposed to get the signatures of the various institutes with which I had been in touch—the library, students' home, etc. In other words it was a certificate to show everything was in order.

When this list was completed (with the exception of a signature from the students' home), I received the last instalment of my grant. Then we went to the Intourist office to book our tickets for the south. It was too late, but they raised no difficulties about giving them to us on Monday. Afterwards I bought quantities of records and books and arrived back at my room pretty exhausted. It was a very hot day too.

Last night I invited my Russian friends Maria, Peter, Alexander and Yuri to a farewell party. We ate bread with goat's cheese and drank aquavit. Peter gave me several books, and Maria presented me with a book and a cigarette case.

When the party broke up, Alexander and Yuri insisted on accompanying Maria and me to the Metro. A pity . . . it meant I didn't have a chance to say goodbye to Maria properly. This was probably an example of the collective spirit—and as good a reason as any for not being wildly enthusiastic about it!

During the evening we had discussed the question of who is more important to society—the physicist or the philologist. The physicists were inclined to think that philologists were of little use to workers and peasants. The whole debate was in the friendliest spirit.

On the way back from the Metro Yuri said he would be interested to hear my impressions of my stay in Moscow. I was pretty careful in what I said, and tried to be polite, but affirmed that in any case Communism was not for me.

He asked if I would be writing about my experiences when I got back to Norway, and at the same time remarked how laughable it was for the Western world to refer to the "slaves of Communism". He pointed to himself and demanded: "Do I look like a slave?"

Then he wanted to know if I had felt myself under any kind of pressure from a dictatorship during my stay—"or perhaps the pressure doesn't affect foreigners?" he added, ironically.

So as usual we got on to the subject of dictatorship and democracy. Yuri produced a spate of words about a classless society, and when I asked for a definition of social classes we finally arrived at the conclusion that one perhaps could after all talk of different classes in the Soviet Union. Classes were determined by many factors—financial and intellectual levels, for instance. They were inherent in all types of society. They could be re-arranged in order of importance, perhaps—or re-arranged into the order of importance as assessed by whatever class had power, but the classes continued to exist.

We agreed that the question was largely one of terminology, but I added that terminology was not so important; facts were.

I told them that if they were interested in what conditions in the Western world were really like, they should visit Norway.

"If we hadn't had a revolution we wouldn't have had this University", Yuri interjected. "My grandfather was a serf, and if the Tsarist régime had continued I wouldn't have been able to study here".

I argued that a bad Tsarist régime still did not justify Communism.

"You are afraid of Communism", Yuri retorted. "But we are satisfied with it and don't want to export it".

I said events in Eastern Europe had made us doubt the truth of that statement. The export of Communism to Czechoslovakia by means of a *coup d'état* was one of the reasons why we had joined NATO.

His reply surprised me. He said he could partly understand that—but that he didn't want to talk about NATO.

Wednesday, June 15

The last few days in Moscow have been a nightmare. Of preparations for the trip. Of dashing from one bureau to another. . .

On Sunday I spent most of the day packing. It's incredible how much stuff one accumulates. In the afternoon I went round saying goodbye to friends.

On Monday I got up early and packed all my books into parcels weighing five kilos each and sent them home by post. It cost almost 100 roubles.

I also tried to send my gramophone records and paint-box, but records can only be sent if packed in wooden boxes weighing no more than three kilos—in a word, impossible.

I shoved my records into a case and propose to drag my paint box around with me. Ingjald and I then set off into town to send off our baggage. As we came out of the University, each carrying two bags, we were stopped by the woman at the door to whom we have to show our passes every time we enter. She informed us that it was necessary to have a special permit to take bags out of the University.

This really was the last straw. I let fly with everything I knew . . . and in three minutes we were on our way. We took a taxi to the Registration Bureau, where we were to collect our exit permits and travel permits. The bureau closed at 1 p.m.—and at precisely that time we stormed in and got what we had come for.

Some of the Americans who had tried to get their exit visas before leaving on their trip had been refused, so it is clear we continue to be "better than the Americans".

We made our way to Leningrad Station (Moscow) in order to send our bags and my skis back home via Leningrad. It took hours to track down the parcels office. Then when we found it they refused to despatch the bags unless they were properly locked. After another hunt we found a man who could put metal bands around them.

Back at the parcels office we were told that the baggage could not be sent direct to Norway, so everything has to go to Leningrad. When all this had been fixed they informed us that it will cost between four and five roubles per parcel per day to store them in Leningrad. As we cannot pick them up for almost three weeks this will run into a pretty hefty sum. Finally we arranged with the clerk that the baggage would not be sent from Moscow until June 30.

I think the whole thing is bound to go haywire somewhere along the line, but we can only keep our fingers crossed and hope for the best.

Then the porter who had carried our bags five metres asked for 30 roubles—and got 10. He had to have 30 roubles, he said, to make up the price of a bottle of vodka. To crown it all, we had to run round for three quarters of an hour looking for the place to pay the cost of the freight. That was 70 roubles.

I went off to see Alexeev to pick up the certificates he had promised me. He kept me waiting for half and hour—and then only to complain about the heat and to regret that he was unable to do any work in such a temperature. I would have to call again later in the day.

Meanwhile, Ingjald had been to the Intourist offices to get our tickets for the trip south. That morning we had received three chits from the Foreign Bureau—one for air tickets, one for train tickets, and one for hotel reservations. I had fetched them myself, and had failed to notice that the chit concerning air tickets only applied to the stretch from the Crimea to Kiev and Leningrad and not for the journey between Moscow and the Caucasus —as had been agreed with Nikoforov. Instead we had been given a chit for a train journey from Moscow to the Caucasus. We both thought there had been a mistake, and after a certain amount of shouting Ingjald managed to wrest the appropriate air tickets out of Intourist without the relevant paper from Nikoforov.

The route was via Minvody, and we had been told earlier that after a stop in Minvody there would be a plane from there to Ordzhonikidze, from which point we would proceed to the Caucasus. We had built our travel plans on this basis, but now it transpired there was no air route from Minvody to Ordzhonikidze, which would delay us for one day. But there was nothing to be done, even though it would play havoc with our hotel reservations.

Ingjald and I linked up at the Intourist Head Office to book our hotel rooms. But naturally we couldn't fix things up as easily as that. They would only accept notification from Nikoforov and told us to ring up later. The situation doesn't seem too bright.

When I phoned later in the day they simply told me to ring back next day. I explained that by then I proposed to be in the Caucasus so that what they wanted would be difficult. We compromised. I would phone early in the morning.

Thursday, June 16

On the day of our departure we got up early, cleaned the flat and packed the few things we proposed to take with us—naturally this was more than we'd intended. In the middle of all this we had a call from the Foreign Bureau. It was to tell me I was wanted immediately. I went along and was ushered in straight away to see Nikoforov, who was polite but far from pleasant.

He had been informed, he said, that we had bought air tickets to Minvody instead of train tickets to Ordzhonikidze, as had been stipulated in the paper from his office. How had this happened?

I replied truthfully that it had been agreed we should fly in the first place, so that naturally I thought a mistake had been made. Nikoforov retorted that there had been no mistake, and furthermore that he was astonished that we had been allowed to buy air tickets without a note from him.

The reason we had to travel the whole distance by rail was that the road between Minvody and Ordzhonikidze was under repair. The only possible way of getting from Minvody to Ordzhonikidze was therefore to take a train, but as this was a long and difficult journey Nikoforov had thought it better for us to do the whole trip by rail (it means two days in the train, at least). Now we would have to go and exchange our air tickets for rail tickets, he said.

I explained meekly that this might cause some difficulty since the plane we were supposed to be taking would be leaving in a couple of hours. Nikoforov said that despite the fact that we had only ourselves to blame for this mess, he would do his best to help us.

Without the least confidence in his words I went into the outer office to get the proper paper. Five minutes later, however, I was called back into Nikoforov's room and told we could, after all, fly to Minvody, but would have to go by train from there to Ordzhonikidze.

I swore to do this on my honour, and as I left the room Nikoforov followed me with a Parthian shot —"Always read through the papers you are given".

Another session of washing and packing, and finally we went into town by taxi. I phoned Intourist Head Office again to ask about the hotel reservations. I told them who I was and what the

Sejersted stands in the gardens of the former Tsarist summer palace at Yalta, scene of the famous Yalta Conference now a workers' convalescent home. Below: the author with baggage sent too soon from Moscow.

call was about. Ring again later—after lunch, they said. I explained that this was out of the question, that I'd been promised reservations, and that I was leaving in a quarter of an hour.

The woman at the other end again asked who I was. When I'd repeated it a couple of times with the utmost clarity she suddenly announced that the rooms had in fact been booked. That was all I wanted to know. It was one worry less as we took a cab out to Vnukovo airfield.

We ate at the airfield cafeteria and wandered around for a time. It was pretty obvious that we were being watched by a civilian in a yellow shirt—one time when our suspicions weren't unfounded. At 1.45 p.m. however, we were airborne in a small twin-engined aircraft, and about two-and-a-half-hours later we flew over Kharkov. Low cloud had largely obscured the view from the plane most of the time. We ate in the airport restaurant at Kharkov, and just as we were about to take off again Ingjald held everything up while he retrieved his fountain pen from the restaurant.

At about 5 p.m. we were off again, and beneath us an unending plain, almost treeless, yawned as far as the eye could see. Seen from above it was a pretty barren and gloomy picture.

We landed in Rostov after a flight of about one-and-a-half-hours, and were due to leave again half an hour later. But the take-off was delayed while the following little scene was played out. . . .

A large plane touched down and out of it stepped a couple of fat men. They were received by another group of fat men. Handshakes all round, then the group went off to some cars and dashed away at high speed. A small crowd had collected to watch and I asked what it was all about. A man told me that a party VIP had just arrived—Aristov of the Soviet Presidium. He had been met by Kirichenko, who was now General Secretary of the Party in the Rostov district—after having been removed from the Presidium. Nobody knew what Aristov was doing in Rostov.

We left Rostov later, but after flying for about an hour had to turn back as there was a thunderstorm at Minvody. We were escorted to the Intourist wing of the airport and given a comfortable room. The "ordinary" passengers had to make their own arrangements about shelter for the night, which didn't noticeably improve my appreciation of this wonderful classless society!

A fat general occupied the room next to us.

Our plane was scheduled to leave around four o'clock in the morning, but we heard that a little later there would be a plane direct to Ordzhonikidze, which would suit us admirably. We tried to change our tickets but couldn't manage it because nobody could find out if there were any vacant seats on the aircraft.

So we were stuck with the Minvody trip. As we flew there we could see the sombre Caucasian mountains rearing up from the dreary Russian steppes like a fantasy in perspective. A marvellous sight. And there, a giant among giants, was Mount Elbrus, bathed in morning sunlight.

At Minvody airport we were met by a young man from the airline. He told us in very bad English that he had received a telegram from Moscow announcing our arrival and that it would be his pleasure and privilege to show us to the railway station, a sort of hail and farewell in the same breath. Despite the fact that we spoke Russian the whole time, he insisted on airing his execrable

English.

On arrival at the station we discovered that the first train did not leave for three hours, so we sat down in a park and went to sleep. The train journey was the hottest thing I have ever experienced, and it took no less than five hours. Even then the train did not go into Ordzhonikidze. We had to get off at a station about 30 kilometres outside and take a taxi. This we shared with a rather attractive girl of Asiatic appearance.

To our great astonishment we found that we were expected at the hotel, despite the fact that our itinerary did not include a night stop in Ordzhonikidze. According to plan we should have arrived there that morning and left almost immediately by bus through the Caucasus. By having to stay overnight we would lose one day.

In the hotel we met some of our fellow-passengers from the plane who had arrived by taxi on the road which—according to Nikiforov—"was under repair".

In the afternoon we took a look at the town—in the company of a nice Intourist representative—a 26-year-old girl. We saw the celebrated mountain river Cherek which runs through the town. This river, which has been praised in song and story, didn't look very romantic to us. It looked unpleasantly filthy.

Next morning we crept into a dirty old crock of a bus which groaned its way to Tiflis in eight-and-a-half-hours. The road was terrible but the scenery beautiful. On a Caucasian summit we washed in snow and drank the mineral water that gushed from the mountain. Our fellow passengers on the bus were all local people, and all the men sported moustaches.

At the Intourist Hotel in Tiflis they were pretty unpleasant and said they had never heard of us. We managed to get hold of a young man in the office who was kind enough to inquire at another big hotel—the Tblisi. It turned out that they were expecting us at the Tblisi, which is where I am writing this. It is very hot indeed today and I'm beginning to feel fagged out.

Sunday, June 19

We toured Tiflis on Friday. Almost as soon as we went into the street we had the good fortune to get into conversation with a philologist who became our guide for the rest of the day. The Georgians are extremely approachable and unbelievably hospitable. Even absolute strangers were insisting on paying our bus fares.

By and large things seem very different here from what they are in sombre Russia. Our guide told us that some authorities didn't like people to go around with foreigners. He shrugged. "That's too bad", he said. One gets the impression that people live far more naturally in this part of the world.

We went first to the old part of the city, with its cathedral and ancient ruined fortress perched on a hill. Then we pottered around in the beautiful botanical gardens.

When we got back to the hotel we booked air tickets to Sukhum. We were still thinking about that train journey from Minvody. We didn't want anything like that again at any price. We also cabled our hotel in Sukhum in order to make sure of rooms when we arrived.

One of our Georgian friends in Moscow had

given us the address of her family in Tiflis, so Ingjald phoned up and spoke to her sister. She invited us home the same day but we were unable to go since we'd already arranged to spend some time with a young man we had met on the bus.

He rang us this morning at the hotel and we arranged to meet at 5 p.m. We waited but he failed to appear, so Ingjald and I took the funicular up the mountain, where there was a splendid restaurant and a wonderful view.

Early next morning we went to the airport, after a little scene in the hotel. They tried to charge us for an extra day, but that trick failed to come off. The plane took off about an hour late. No apology. No explanation. We stopped once en route, and round mid-day arrived in Sukhum.

The hotel was excellent. It faced the seaside promenade, which is flanked with palm trees. We were also expected here. Yesterday the weather was perfect and we spent several hours on the beach, with the temperature of the water at 22 deg C. In the evening there was a dance and considerable festivity in the hotel roof-garden. When we arrived a Norwegian flag had been placed on our table. We got into conversation with some local students who supplied us with vast quantities of champagne. Finally, the waiter arrived with two litre bottles of wine sent to us from someone at a nearby table. In all—a jolly good evening.

Today's report: Mild, tropical rain—and a slight hangover.

We have fixed up a sight-seeing tour with one of our friends of last night.

On Sunday we met our friend Oleg, and took a look at the municipal monkey station—this being a scientific institute where they conduct experiments with apes. It is the outstanding feature of the town. Then we visited the botanical gardens, where everything was unbelievably lush.

After the tour we called on Oleg's cousin, a doctor who lives in a very nice little flat in the town centre. He had two sweet children who sat as if nailed in front of a TV set. Gradually various friends dropped in, including a football enthusiast with a moustache who talked about Ingemar Johannson, the Swedish boxer.

We were regaled with a tremendous dinner and quantities of highly-spiced Georgian wine. The meal started with everyone draining a large tumbler of vodka—this was absolutely obligatory. Then we had one more glass (on empty stomachs!) before starting on the meal and the home-made wines, which were drunk from something like a whisky glass and had to be put down in one sharp gulp.

We found ourselves drinking several toasts to Stalin, whose portrait hung on the wall, and the entire company (ourselves excepted), got tears in their eyes each time. Then we drank toasts to the various members of the family, and ended up by toasting Khrushchev and all his henchmen. In between there were other odd toasts—to peace and friendship, liberty, etc. To avoid a complete scandal I was compelled to get to my feet and make a snuffling sort of speech of thanks, after which the party broke up and we managed—somehow—to get back to the hotel.

The next evening—Monday—we boarded a nice little boat called the *Abchasiya*, which delivered us to Sochi next morning. On the quay we caught an Intourist bus along with a large group of Germans. They had never heard of us at the Intourist hotel, but eventually it was discovered that we had been booked in at another place—the Primorskaya—which is a very decent hotel.

We went straight off for a swim, and found the beach packed. Everybody has the same idea in this weather. As soon as we arrived back at the hotel we were asked to call at the Intourist Bureau, where an elderly woman told us off for not having visited her immediately we arrived. She pointed out that our reservations had been made solely on the basis of the telegram we had sent from Sukhum, and she had heard nothing from Moscow about us.

She went on that as our route had been planned in Moscow the shipping company must already have booked us on to Yalta. We explained at great length that we didn't want reserved places—we wished to remain flexible in our travels. According to our Moscow plan we should have left Sochi on June 23—the next day—but we asked the old girl to book us tickets for the 25th instead as we had found Sochi such a lovely place.

She didn't like this at all. She said there were certainly no vacant places for the 25th—only on the 23rd—so that was that.

Saturday, June 25

We left Sochi on June 23 after all, in spite of efforts to prolong our stay. Our last act at the hotel was to have a serious quarrel with an incredibly sour female receptionist who demanded payment for a day longer than we had stayed. This is the second time they've tried this during our trip.

On the morning of June 23 we boarded the

passenger boat *Gruziya*. Soon after lunch we called at Tuapse where it was frightfully hot and equally boring, and in the evening arrived in Novorossisk. There I sent a cable to friends of mine who were getting married in Oslo—it set me back 36 roubles. We saw a Greek and an Italian ship in the harbour, but no Norwegian ships.

Early on June 24 we arrived in Yalta, where everything at the hotel went smoothly. We have booked for four days, which will enable us to take things easily. This, incidentally, is the first hotel that has asked for our passports as well as for our residence and travel permits.

The town is very beautiful, lying encircled by high mountains. It reminds one rather of the South of France. The harbour is small, with a pier just about large enough to take a couple of smallish ships.

Quite a number of Germans and Americans are staying at this hotel. The Americans are obviously here to follow in the footsteps of the late President Roosevelt, who attended the famous Yalta Conference in 1945.

Wednesday, June 29

Now we're in Kiev—miles away from our original schedule and rather pleased with ourselves for having escaped from the confinement of our itinerary.

The last few days have been pretty interesting. It was fine in Yalta on Sunday and Monday, and we spent several pleasant hours on the golden beach a short distance from the town. On Saturday evening

Leningrad . . . and the museum (above) sets out to show how science has disproved the existence of God. Below: The Hermitage, former winter palace of the Tsars, is now an art gallery.

we got talking to a couple of youngish East German tourists and two Russian students. Naturally we discussed politics. One of the Germans asked the Russians what views the Soviet Union had about Germany. The Russians replied that they viewed West Germany with increasing scepticism and thought fascism was getting a hold again. On the other hand they had the greatest confidence in East Germany, and the ties between the countries were close. Soviet relations with East Germany, they said, were much better than with Poland, which continued to show traces of capitalism. So far as the Russians knew, the entire population of East Germany supported the present régime.

They were pretty shaken when one of the East Germans said they were greatly mistaken. And then, far from praising their homeland, the East Germans started boasting about West Germany. One, an accountant, told Ingjald afterwards that when they returned home they would have to write a report for the authorities about everything they had done in the Soviet Union.

On the following day we saw one of the more aggressive Russians again. He was a student of economics at Moscow University. During a long conversation he told us he simply couldn't understand why such marked class differences should exist in the Soviet Union. He was a convinced Communist, he said, and realised that different classes in capitalist countries were inevitable. But why on earth should the Soviet Union follow the same pattern?

Returning from the beach on Sunday we walked through the colossal sanatorium where the Yalta Conference was held. On the way there we lost our way and ran into a heavily guarded gateway. We gathered that this gate led to the summer houses of members of the government—it seems that the Yalta climate suits the present leaders as much as it did the Tsars.

On Tuesday we were up early to pack our bags. As we were leaving we encountered a familiar group of American students who had arrived that morning from Moscow. We were delighted to see them again. They told us that Nikoforov, who was supposed to have accompanied them, had called it off the morning they were due to leave Moscow. Instead they had been supplied with two unknown "interpreters".

They were only moderately pleased with their trip so far. The most interesting place they had seen was Erevan—from which town their departure had been rather dramatic. The evening before they were due to leave they were suddenly told to pack up. Then they were stowed into a bus which bumped along a terrible road to Tiflis throughout the night. No apologies. No explanation.

We had to say a hasty goodbye to our American friends and rush to the Intourist car that was to take us to the heliport—a small area about ten minutes north-east of the town. The helicopter was full, and its eleven passengers included an American.

We flew south-west along the coast to a place where the Caucasian mountain range was probably lower. We were so far west that we could make out Bakhchisarai, ancient seat of the Tartar Khan. In half an hour we landed at Simferopol, where we had to wait three or four hours for a plane to Kiev.

Over lunch in the airport restaurant we talked to a Russian seaman from a whaler. He was at our table having his own form of lunch—mostly vodka. He had just signed off in Odessa and was on his way home to Kiev. He told us that the heli-copter in which we arrived was used during the winter months by whaling expeditions for spotting purposes. He also said he'd once visited Norway—as a member of a crew collecting a refrigerator ship. As a parting gift he gave us a peace-pin.

The plane to Kiev was a TU-104. We flew at about 8,000 metres and at a speed of over 800 km per hour. Consequently it took only about an hour to Kiev. Cloud obscured some of the view, though we could make out parts of the Sea of Azov.

The airfield east of Kiev was evidently a military one. Vast numbers of fighter planes were lined up there. We climbed into an unpleasantly warm bus which took about an hour to get us into town. We went into the Intourist hotel full of anxiety that there might be no accommodation. Nikoforov had warned us about this possibility, and we had neglected to send a telegram saying we were coming. To our surprise we mentioned only that we were Norwegian students—and got a room straight away.

Even though we're miles away from our original schedule the bush telegraph must be functioning very well indeed!

Kiev seems a charming and very pretty town. Today we visited the famous monastery here. One of the buildings houses an exhibition designed to demonstrate how science has disproved religion. A big play is made of Soviet space achievements along the lines that none of the sputniks they have sent up has yet discovered this mythical place called heaven. One of the exhibition's little treasures is a photo-graph of a gold telephone which, it is alleged, had been presented by the American "imperialists" to the Vatican.

Friday, July 1

Our time is running out. . . . On Sunday morning (July 3) we shall be leaving by train for Helsinki and home.

Yesterday morning we packed again and left Kiev by jet aircraft for Leningrad. The weather was pretty uncertain, with lots of cloud. About 20 minutes before landing we caught sight of what must have been Lake Peipus. The whole trip took one and three quarter hours, which isn't bad going.

We got a room at the Hotel Europa in Leningrad without trouble, and went to the railway station to inquire about our luggage (we had been a bit worried about this during the trip; I was certain something would go wrong at the Moscow end). But there they were! Only one thing was wrong. They had arrived as early as June 14, which meant they had been waiting in Leningrad for two and a half weeks accumulating extra charges. In fact these came to 48 roubles, which we were very reluctant to pay. We were told we could have a word with "the boss" next day.

Today we booked our tickets for Helsinki. It was impossible to book any farther than this—we were assured nobody in Leningrad could tell us about boats between Helsinki and Stockholm. Then we went to the station and talked to "the boss" so convincingly that we didn't have to pay anything to collect the luggage. We took it along to the left-luggage office, where at first they refused to receive it on the grounds that there was no room. But I behaved as though I didn't understand a word they were saying, and eventually they took the luggage just to get rid of us.

The high spot of our stay in Leningrad was the

128

visit to the Hermitage—the old winter palace of the Tsars. This was a fabulous place, and I saw the most beautiful Matisse pictures I have ever set eyes on.

POSTSCRIPT

Russia is behind us now, but my mind whirls with vivid memories. On the train out of Leningrad on Sunday morning (July 3) we had half a coach to ourselves, so we were able to take our vast quantities of luggage into the compartment with us. There was a party of Russians in the coach —they were getting out of the Soviet paradise for the first time and were as inquisitive as children.

There was no trouble at the customs. They didn't ask us to open any of the bags, but the inspector did leaf through the books he found. In one of them he came across my diary, and I held my breath while he studied it with evident interest.

Finally we crossed into Finland, and there was a sudden, inexplicable feeling of relief. Not that anything sinister had happened, or even anything worth protesting about. It was perhaps the relief of re-entering a world more in tune with the way we thought, a world in which we could recognise phrases like peace and freedom without feeling that they had been adjusted to fit a particular set of circumstances and could be altered tomorrow by special decree.

This was our world, and in returning it seemed as though we had crossed a tremendous ideological chasm.